About the Author

Noel Stewart is also the author of, *ETHICS: An Introduction to Moral Philosophy* (Polity, 2008).

He used to be a sincere Christian — so sincere, he attended Bible college, becoming assistant pastor in a Pentecostal church.

But he had to give all that up when he finally saw the light.

Voltaire helped him laugh his way out.

For those still in, I hope this book helps them laugh their way out too.

For those half out, may it help them laugh their way even further out.

And for those completely out, may it simply make them laugh.

The Jesus Interviews
(A Sceptical Entertainment)

Noel Stewart

The Jesus Interviews
(A Sceptical Entertainment)

Olympia Publishers
London

www.olympiapublishers.com

OLYMPIA PAPERBACK EDITION

A CIP catalogue record for this title is
available from the British Library.

ISBN: 978-1-78830-790-1

This is a work of fiction.
Names, characters, places and incidents originate from the writer's
imagination. Any resemblance to actual persons, living or dead, is
purely coincidental.

First Published in 2020

Olympia Publishers
Tallis House
2 Tallis Street
London
EC4Y 0AB

Printed in Great Britain

Dedication

Written in honour of my favourite comedian,
the Holy Ghost — a clown of the first rank.

Acknowledgements

Many thanks to the following ornaments to humanity for encouraging me in this sinful endeavour.

My daughter Anna and husband Stu.

My son Simon.

My daughter Alex and partner Fletch.

My wee sis Alison, along with her son Patrick, daughter Danielle and son-in-law Lewis.

My wee sis-in-law Diane.

And from the world of chess, *International Master* Richard Palliser.

Finally, my thanks go to my good neighbour, Sylvia Corsham.

Contents

Introduction

Ask my brother am I a liar. (A Belfast saying)

Imagine you were born 2000 years from now.

Now imagine that no physical evidence of Hitler remains: no archive footage, no war diaries, no government documents, no documentaries, no recorded interviews, no copies of *Mein Kampf*, no photographs, and so on.

Now imagine that *all* we know of Hitler in 2000 years' time is based on just *four* written accounts, *none* of which were written until about forty to seventy years after Hitler's death, and *all* of which were written, not by mere Nazi sympathisers, but by SS men.

How much would you trust those accounts?

Keep this thought in your head the next time you read the gospels.

Matthew. 1:18 – 2:23 and Luke. 2: 1 – 20

I was born under a wandering star

Peremy Jaxman: Ladies and gentlemen, we are indeed fortunate to have none other than Jesus Christ as our guest on the show tonight, so will you please give a big welcome to the Son of God!

(Loud applause as Jesus comes on stage and sits down; walk-on music is 'I was born under a wandering star' by Lee Marvin, from 'Paint your Wagon'.)

PJ: Welcome to the studio Jesus. Thank you so much for coming.

Jesus: Hello Peremy; it's good to be here.

PJ: I'd like to devote this interview to the events surrounding your birth. Of all the millions of babies born throughout history, the story of your birth is probably the most famous and fascinating, and I was hoping you'd be able to clear up some of the puzzles surrounding it.

J: Puzzles? I didn't think there *were* any. Stable, star, Wise Men, shepherds — it all seems pretty straightforward to me.

PJ: Splendid! Then you'll be able to set us all straight about what happened. I'd like to start by taking you back nine months before the stable. It all starts when your mum Mary gets pregnant by the Holy Ghost.

J: That's right, but she didn't tell my stepdad, Joe.

PJ: Can you blame her? He'd have to be an idiot to swallow a story like that on just her say-so.

J: True. That's why it took nothing less than a dream to convince him.

PJ: A dream, eh? That's cast-iron proof in anyone's book.

J: Yeah; my heavenly Father pulled out all the stops to get Joe on board.

PJ: So, I take it that in the dream, God told Joe that the Holy Ghost... er... diddled his fiancée before he did.

J: I suppose so, but I wouldn't put it quite like that.

PJ: Why not? Don't you think the Holy Ghost enjoyed it?

J: Absolutely not!

PJ: Oh? Wasn't your mum hot?

J: What can I say? Boys don't think about their mums that way.

PJ: You haven't read Freud then.

J: Who?

PJ: Oh, nothing.

J: The main thing was simply to make a baby, so the whole thing was purely functional.

PJ: Wow! The Holy Ghost must be a real pro!

J: Can we talk about something else?

PJ: Of course. Now, about your stepdad; don't you think we should spare a thought for him?

J: How do you mean?

PJ: Well, put yourself in his shoes. There he is — never had sex, but now he's all fired up because he's soon going to have the greatest sex of his life — and then he learns that God's already done the business with his girl. How would *you* feel? And to make matters worse, he can't have sex for the next nine months because, well, GOD'S IN THERE!

J: I'd never really thought of it from his point of view.

PJ: After that first horrible dream, do you think God the Father gave Joe some, you know, *very special dreams* to tide him over?

J: Well, if he did, they weren't mentioned in the gospel stories.

PJ: And no wonder; it's not the kind of thing that would go down well (if you'll pardon the expression) in a kiddies' Nativity play.

J: Hey, that's my family you're talking about!

PJ: And a unique family it is too — three dads and a mum who's still a virgin. Have you thought about therapy?

J: But there's nothing wrong with me. Why would I need therapy?

PJ: You know... the old God-complex. You *think* you're God.

J: (emphatically) But I *am* God!

PJ: (putting his hand on Jesus's arm in a reassuring yet utterly condescending way) ... Of *course* you are... Now, I want to ask you about the three Wise Guys from the East. What's the deal with that star?

J: Oh, you mean the Nat Nav?

PJ: Nat Nav?

J: Yes, Nativity Navigation System. I call it Nat Nav for short. Great idea, don't you think?

PJ: Yeah, if it worked.

J: What are you getting at?

PJ: By following your Nat Nav contraption the Wise Guys ended up in Jerusalem, not Bethlehem. That's six miles off course.

J: Well, it was a prototype and we had a few teething troubles.

PJ: I understand. We had the same sort of problems with our modern version. It's just that I expect God to do a better job. I mean, it didn't just take them to the wrong street; it was the wrong town!

J: Well, to tell you the truth, there's another side to these teething troubles. You see, God the Father needed the Wise Men to end up in Jerusalem so they could tell Herod about me being born the new king of the Jews.

PJ: Why does he want Herod to know?

J: So that the Old Testament prophecy about the murdered children would be fulfilled.

PJ: What!?

J: Yes, you see there was a prophecy about lots of children being murdered around the time of my birth, and the best way of fulfilling this was for Herod to do it, so he needed to find out about my birth.

PJ: Are you telling me that the Nat Nav was deliberately sabotaged by God the Father so it would mislead the Wise Guys to Jerusalem to make sure a prophecy about murdered babies would come true!?

J: I know it looks bad but…

PJ: But why the prophecy in the first place?

J: It's a mystery. Ask the Holy Ghost; he wrote it.

PJ: Couldn't it just not have been written?

J: Apparently not.

PJ: So, Herod killed them all because he was trying to kill you. How did you escape?

J: Joe got another one of his dreams to warn him, so we upped sticks and moved to Egypt right after the Wise Guys and shepherds left.

PJ: And none of the parents of the other kids got a dream?

J: No.

PJ: So the prophecy the Holy Ghost wrote could come true?

J: Yes.

PJ: Boy, the Holy Ghost just hates to be wrong, doesn't he?

J: Doesn't everyone?

PJ: True, but unlike him, most people would draw the line at murdering children. Anyway, let's get back to Jerusalem where the three Wise Guys have just arrived. I've read Matthew's account and I just don't get it.

J: What don't you get?

PJ: Well, Herod badly wants you dead. A new king is a threat. These Wise Guys breeze into town looking for this new-born king. He pretends he wants to worship this king too, so he asks them to return from Bethlehem once they've found you and tell him where you are.

J: Fine so far. What's your problem?

PJ: Well, Herod's a smart cookie. Not much gets past him. What I don't get is why he didn't have a couple of his goons tail the Wise Guys instead of naively trusting them to return and tell him the truth. But no, he lets them waltz out of his palace on their own. How could he be so stupid?

J: Maybe God melted his brain.

PJ: Did he melt his eyes too?

J: What do you mean?

PJ: Well, while the Wise Guys were in Jerusalem, your brain-melting heavenly Father got the Nat Nav working again, so the Wise Guys were able to follow the star from Jerusalem to the stable in Bethlehem. All Herod had to do was open his eyes and follow the star and it would have led him straight to you. Why didn't he do that?

J: Mmm… Maybe only the Wise Guys could see the star.

PJ: You mean it was all in their minds? Wow! I wonder what they were on.

J: What makes you think they were on anything?

PJ: They're seeing stars, dude; they're from *The East*, man; you know… *The East* — a lot of weird shit growing out there.

J: I wouldn't know.

PJ: Of course; you were just a foetus at the time.

J: 'Baby' sounds better. 'The foetus Jesus' just doesn't have the same ring to it.

PJ: Good point. Now, let's move on to the prezzies. They seem a bit thoughtless. I mean, a kid can only have so much fun with myrrh.

J: (wistfully) Yeah… I'd always wanted a 'Junior Joiner Outfit'; but it never happened.

PJ: What about the gold? Couldn't Joe have used that to buy you something?

J: You'd think, but I suppose he needed it to pay the bills. Kids don't come cheap, and his carpentry business was going down the toilet, what with all the travelling. Have *you* ever tried making a wardrobe on the back of a donkey?

PJ: Didn't business pick up when the family moved to Egypt?

J: Not really; he just couldn't get them interested in wooden pyramids.

PJ: What about the frankincense? That's supposed to be pretty expensive perfume isn't it? Couldn't Joe have sold that?

J: No. It was used up in no time. That stable reeked, the donkey stank, and then there were the nappies... Let's just say it came in handy as an air freshener.

PJ: Any luck with the myrrh?

J: No, no takers.

PJ: Can't say I'm surprised. Nobody knows what the hell that stuff is anyway... now, the Wise guys weren't your only visitors that night. I'd like to ask you about the shepherds if I may.

J: Yes, of course; you know, they call me 'The Good Shepherd'.

PJ: So I've heard. But these were pretty second-rate shepherds, if you ask me.

J: Why do you say that?

PJ: Well, once the heavenly choir beat it back to heaven after singing your praises, the shepherds all downed tools and ran off to find you. What worries me is the sheep.

J: What do you mean?

PJ: Who was looking after them? They could have been rustled, or eaten by wolves.

J: I'm sure they were okay; my heavenly Father would have looked after them.

PJ: Yeah, just like he looked after those murdered children. Those shepherds were out there for a reason.

J: Aren't you missing the big picture here?

PJ: Ah yes; I was forgetting. This is all about *you*, isn't it? Okay then, maybe you could explain how the shepherds found the stable. Unlike the Wise Guys, they didn't have access to your Nat Nav, and there was no 'Bethlehem A-Z' back then.

J: Maybe they bumped into the Wise Guys on the way.

PJ: With them all there together the stable must have been heaving. I bet that frankincense was working overtime. So, what prezzies did the shepherds give you?

J: None.

PJ: Not even a toy sheep?

J: No.

PJ: Gift voucher?

J: Nope.

PJ: How embarrassing. I bet the Wise Guys looked pretty smug.

J: Who cares? The shepherds brought nothing at all, and the Wise Guys brought nothing for *me*. Either way, I got no prezzies.

PJ: I know. And we all feel for you. No child should be without prezzies at Christmas, so to make it up to you, we've all clubbed together to buy you a present.

J: Oooh! What is it?

PJ: (proudly hands over the present wrapped up) It's a state-of-the-art wine-making kit.

J: (Jesus unwraps it to reveal a bottle.) (Looks at it glumly) … But this is just water.

PJ: Exactly!

J: Thanks a million.

PJ: You're welcome. And now, alas, our time's run out. Jesus, thank you so much for being our guest tonight. Jesus Christ, ladies and gentlemen! (Applause).

[Fade out to Bowie singing 'Starman']

John. 2: 1 – 11

The Chianti-Christ

(Enthusiastic applause as Peremy and Jesus come on stage and sit down; walk-on music is 'The Drinking Song' by Mario Lanza, from 'The Student Prince'.)

Peremy Jaxman (PJ): A very warm welcome to the show, Jesus.

Jesus (J): Thanks, Peremy; it's a joy to be here.

PJ: Wonderful! Now Jesus, of the many miracles you performed, some have had a particular fascination for people of every era. Tonight, if I may, I'd like to ask you a few questions about one of these — the first one, where you turned water into wine.

J: Ah yes. That was some wedding party! You know, normally I can remember my miracles very clearly, but for some reason that one's a bit hazy…

PJ: Yes, I can imagine… Anyway, please try to remember what you can. I'd like to start by asking whether you had a particular percentage proof in mind.

J: No, not as such, but being my debut miracle, I wanted to get off to a flying start.

PJ: And I think you succeeded! I mean, the guests were *already* well-oiled by the time the first lot of wine ran out, but when the chief steward tasted *your* concoction, he congratulated the bridegroom for saving the *best* wine till last!

J: Yes, well it was good stuff — the sort that puts hairs on your chest and parts them down the middle. And the funny thing was, they didn't know it was me that did it... hee hee.

PJ: So, to be clear, are you saying it was *not* alcohol-free?

J: Pilleeeze! Some guests were still in rehab three months later.

PJ: Cool! So, would you describe yourself as a party animal?

J: Not really.

PJ: What about karaoke?

J: You're kidding, right?

PJ: (Making a note and reading it to himself — "don't ask him to sing 'My Way' at the end of the show"). Okay, but it's fair to say that you're a handy man to have around when the beer goes flat.

J: I suppose so, but a Messiah's job is not to get parties back on their feet.

PJ: That's true. When your mum Mary realised the wine had run out...

J: I don't call her 'Mary'.

PJ: I beg your pardon. When *Holy* Mary was showing concern about the lack of wine...

J: I don't call her that either.

PJ: That's right. You call her 'Woman'. Doesn't that strike you as odd? You don't seem very close. Is it a difficult relationship?

J: I'd rather not talk about it.

PJ: I noticed that in John's gospel it says nothing about Joseph being at the party, so…

J: I don't call him 'Joseph'.

PJ: Let me guess; 'Holy Joe'?

J: No.

PJ: What about 'Man'?

J: What's it to you that he wasn't there?

PJ: I just thought that maybe 'Man' wasn't in the picture any more, and that being stuck at home with 'Woman' was beginning to get on your nerves.

J: Why would you think that?

PJ: Oh, I don't know… you're thirty, single, still living with your mum. I thought maybe your Messiah wheeze was simply your way of getting out of the house.

J: No. Can we move on?

PJ: Of course. What do you say to critics who call you a mummy's boy?

J: I'd say that I was the Son of my Father in heaven.

PJ: So, you're a daddy's boy.

J: What was your question?

PJ: Ah yes; I was saying that your mum came over to you, concerned that there was no more booze. Does she like a drink?

J: She's not a lush if that's what you mean.

PJ: I see… Not a 'good time gal', eh? She was just worried the party was on the slide, that's all. Now, you told her she shouldn't have involved you—your time had not yet come. It seems she was poking her nose in where it didn't belong. Do you think she wanted to be your manager?

J: Messiahs don't have managers.

PJ: Your agent then?

J: I did it as a favour to her and the party organisers.

PJ: It still looks like you were bounced into it by your mum.

J: Not exactly. I simply responded to a party crisis.

PJ: Do you regret the theological problems it raises?

J: How do you mean?

PJ: You know, with Saint Paul saying that drunks won't go to heaven. This seems to be at odds with what can only be described as your encouragement of binge drinking. Were the partygoers from Ireland by any chance?

J: Where?

PJ: Never mind. The point is, Paul hates drunks, yet here you are, holding a happy hour with the drinks on you.

J: You've missed the point of the miracle. It was all symbolic you know.

PJ: You don't say!

J: Yes; you see, the water represents the old second-rate covenant of the Old Testament where everyone had the drudgery of obeying the ten commandments in order to get into heaven. But the wine represents the new covenant of the New Testament where no one has to actually *do* anything to get to heaven except simply have faith in me. It's less of a drag.

PJ: And that's your excuse for getting a couple of hundred people legless?

J: Well, it worked. John's gospel says that by doing this I revealed my glory.

PJ: I'm sure no one would deny that downing 600 litres of top-notch liquor must have indeed been glorious…

J: It wasn't done just for the glory. It was from that very moment my disciples had faith in me and followed me around.

PJ: And no wonder; you're a walking drinks cabinet.

J: It wasn't like that… they saw the symbolism.

PJ: Yes of course; that's what they saw—not free drinks for life. Now, there's another theological problem.

J: (Despairingly) Not another one?

PJ: I'm afraid so; it's to do with using the stupendous power of God just to liven up a party. Why not do something a bit more worthwhile, like curing cancer or stopping the Coronavirus?

J: Suffering is a test. Try to overcome suffering with joy by thinking of happier things.

PJ: Okay, I'll try… hmm… How about this? — *"I realise millions of people may have died from Coronavirus, but hey, at least Jesus's party went well!"* Wow! I feel better already!

J: Har-dee-har-har. Look, it was more than just a party. It was all about symbolism. The wine represents—

PJ: Yeah, we already got your spin on the wine. I'd just like to know how much value you place on a human life.

J: Infinite value of course. You know, God's presence was there at the bedside of every Coronavirus victim.

PJ: Really!?? For all the good it did he might as well have been self-isolating.

J: God doesn't do stuff like that.

PJ: I agree. God's got no excuse.

J: I didn't say that. Though God has his reasons for not healing people, he is still with them in their suffering.

PJ: That's pointless if you don't notice he's there. It's as useless as having a million pounds and not knowing you have it. Having the money does you no good at all.

J: But unlike the money, God *can* do you good. He has the power to heal.

PJ: That just makes things worse. He *can* do you good, but he in fact *doesn't* do you good. That's like drowning in a pool in the presence of a lifeguard who *can* save you but *decides not* to, while all the while just standing by watching till you breathe your last.

J: But, as I said before, God has his reasons.

PJ: Well, all I can say is, his reasons had better bloody well be top-notch. I mean, if a lifeguard doesn't save you the only acceptable reasons would be say, if he suddenly had a stroke, or got struck by lightning, or was taken out by a sniper.

J: I have to agree, those are all top-notch reasons!

PJ: But none of them are available to God because he can't be incapacitated in any way, can he?

J: Nope.

PJ: Then that only leaves reasons to do with God's will. So the big question is, "Does he give a shit?"

J: Of course he does!! God loves everybody.

PJ: If that's the case, then I don't get it. God loves us and he's got all power. He *wants* to help; he *can* help; yet he *doesn't* help. So what's stopping him? Why let millions go to the wall every day when he could save them with a miracle?

J: Ah well, God moves in mysterious ways.

PJ: That's a great defence. I'd love to be in court when the lifeguard tries that one. I can picture the scene — Judge: *"You're accused of standing by while a child drowned. How do you plead?"* Lifeguard: *"Not guilty your honour, on the grounds of being mentally mysterious."* Judge: *"I find you guilty."* Lifeguard: *"But why? There's been no trial yet."* Judge: *"I'm also mentally mysterious."*

J: What's your point?

PJ: Appealing to mystery is a cop-out. You can use it to get away with anything.

J: But God's not trying to cop-out. He has *genuine* reasons for not healing people, and they're *really* mysterious.

PJ: You know, it *sounds* like you're saying something new, but these new words don't change a thing.

J: What do you mean?

PJ: Well, let's plug them in to our court case with the lifeguard and see what happens…Lifeguard: *"Not guilty your honour, on the grounds of having* **genuine** *reasons which are* **really** *mysterious."* Judge: *"I find you guilty."* Lifeguard: *"But why? There's been no trial yet."* Judge: *"I have* **genuine** *reasons which are also* **really** *mysterious."* You see? Nothing changes.

J: Well, yes, I can see there's a problem. But there's a difference between human beings and God. You can't trust other people's motives, but you *can* trust God's.

PJ: But his track record doesn't exactly inspire confidence. Why should we trust God?

J: Ah, the thing is, you're not allowed to ask questions like that, because it's a matter of *faith,* and if you ask for *reasons* for trusting God, it undermines the whole business. Faith and reason are not the best of friends.

PJ: *There's* a surprise. So, our job when it comes to the question of God and suffering, is to shut up, not think, and just believe.

J: That's more or less it. God's ways must remain mysterious.

PJ: Would you say they're so mysterious they mystify even you?

J: Not really; God keeps me in the loop. It's just that I can't explain it to **you.**

PJ: So I see. It seems the file on 'God's Ways' has been classified *Top Secret*. Only the politburo of the trinity has access.

J: Yes; it's on a 'need to know' basis, and I'm afraid God doesn't have a 'Freedom of Information' Act you can appeal to.

PJ: It's just as I thought. God's not democratic; he's totalitarian. Well Jesus, thank you so much for *trying* to answer my questions.

J: Not at all. Can I offer you a glass of wine? I made it myself.

PJ: Thanks, don't mind if I do... (To audience) Jesus Christ ladies and gentlemen!

(Fade out to 'Little old wine-drinker me' by Dean Martin.)

Matthew. 15: 21 – 28 and Mark. 7: 24 – 30

Anti-Gentile Jesus Meek and Mild

(Applause as Peremy comes on stage; walk-on music is, 'How much is that doggy in the window?')

PJ: Good evening ladies and gentlemen. I'm sure you're looking forward, as am I, to hearing the Son of God talk a bit more about his amazing life down here on Earth. So, without further ado, will you please give it up for the one and only, Jesus Christ!

(Loud applause as Jesus comes on stage, waves to the crowd, and sits down; walk-on music is, 'I am the one and only' by Chesney Hawkes.)

PJ: Jesus, as you are no doubt aware, your official image is of one who loves all human beings equally. You are renowned the world over for your open-door policy...How does the old hymn go...?

J: "Red and yellow, black and white,

All are precious in my sight."

PJ: That's the one. Well, if you don't mind, I'd like to draw your attention to a little-known incident involving you and a Canaanite woman, which may have a bearing on your image.

J: What about it?

PJ: Well, the problem is that your treatment of this woman seems to undermine your image as a nonracist.

J: Oh yeah? How's that?

PJ: Well, isn't it true that by describing her as Canaanite, Matthew is telling us that she was not a Jew?

J: Yeah, that's true, but why do you ask?

PJ: Well, let me take you through it step by step. She comes to you in deep distress, begging you to have mercy on her because her daughter is possessed by a demon. Can you remember how you responded to her pleas for help?

J: I ignored her.

PJ: So, you give her the cold shoulder. What happens then?

J: My disciples pressured me to send her packing.

PJ: How could they be so callous? Imagine sending a child of God away in despair when you were the only one who could help her. I bet you tore a strip off them for that, eh?

J: Er... not exactly.

PJ: Jesus, please don't tell me you caved in to their pressure.

J: No, I didn't need to cave in...

PJ: That's a relief.

J: Because I *agreed* with them.

PJ: That's not a relief... So, if you agreed with them, what did you do to get rid of her?

J: I told her I only heal Jews.

PJ: Couldn't you have told her straight, instead of sugar-coating it?

J: Actually, I did sugar-coat it. I told her that I was sent only to the lost sheep of the house of Israel.

PJ: Oh, that's good; like a sign at a guest house saying, "We only take lost sheep of the house of Caucasia", instead of "No blacks".

J: Yeah, it looks bad, but it wasn't my fault; that's what God the Father sent me to do.

PJ: Ah, I see…You were only obeying orders… But she still doesn't give up and keeps on begging you to help her. Can you remind us of your reply?

J: Yes; I said, "It is not fair to take the children's food and throw it to the dogs."

PJ: Can you tell us what you meant by that?

J: Yes, well, the Jews are the children; the food is healing; and the dogs are all those who aren't Jewish.

PJ: Including this woman, and 99% of the world.

J: Er… yes, except the figure may be closer to 99.9%

PJ: Marvellous! So, let me get this straight. When this poor woman comes to you, at her wit's end, pleading for help and compassion, you reply with the racist jibe that she's no better than a dog?

J: It sounds really bad put like that, but the thing is, I did heal her daughter in the end.

PJ: True, but only *after* she agreed she was a dog. Is swallowing racist insults the price of healing?

J: No, no. You've got it all wrong. Let me explain.

PJ: I can't wait to hear this.

J: The insult was merely a test of her faith, and she passed the test, so it all turned out well.

PJ: *That's* your explanation? I can see the headline now … [*"Racist insults test Faith,"* claims unemployed joiner.] So, how did she pass your test?

J: By replying, "Yes, Lord, yet even the dogs eat the crumbs that fall from their masters' table."

PJ: So being a dog, she'll be happy with just one crumb of healing… Hey, hang on a minute, that's 'masters' in the plural! That means she wasn't just referring to you, but to *all* Jews as her masters. Are the Jews the master race then?

J: Mmm… I'm sensing that this isn't coming across too well, but it's just her way of talking.

PJ: Yet you didn't correct her. You didn't reassure her that Jew and Gentile are all equal under God, and that she's not an inferior specimen of humanity.

J: Er… no, not as such. I saw her words as a sign of her faith.

PJ: Not as a sign she knew her place?

J: More as a sign of humility.

PJ: Is that what you call it? Others might see them as a sign of desperation, and quick thinking… she'll take whatever insults you throw at her as long as you heal her daughter. It's interesting that none of the Jews you healed had to suffer racist taunts, and despite this, still bounce back with some witty repartee. How come *they* didn't have to jump through all these hoops to get healed?

J: Because the children's food is theirs by *right*. The dogs, on the other hand, have to *earn* it.

PJ: So, the racist insult wasn't a test—you really meant it.

J: It wasn't meant as an insult. It was merely a statement of fact regarding how God favours Jews above other people.

PJ: Have you heard of the Ku Klux Klan?

J: No

PJ: Well, it's merely a statement of fact regarding the Ku Klux Klan that they favour whites over blacks, but that doesn't make it right. Maybe we should change the words of the hymn to, "Red and yellow, black and white,

But God prefers an Israelite."

J: It's true my heavenly Father and I *were* biased back then, but only until Pentecost; and it wasn't as if the Jewish people deserved it. It was done as a reward to Abraham for his faith.

PJ: Are you telling me that that's what gave them pole position in the queue for healing and salvation? What on earth did Abraham do to earn this reward?

J: Don't you know the story? He was fully prepared to kill his son as a human sacrifice simply because God ordered him to.

PJ: You mean he gets a reward for murder!?

J: It's not murder if God tells you to do it.

PJ: Wasn't that the Yorkshire Ripper's defence?

J: Who?

PJ: Doesn't matter... so, Abraham was only obeying orders, just like you.

J: Er... yes.

PJ: Wasn't that Goering's defence?

J: Who?

PJ: Never mind.

J: Actually, God stepped in just in time and stopped the killing. That's because he's a God of love.

PJ: You don't say!? It's all so clear now; God puts Abraham through the wringer, and you do the same to this woman, and all because of love.

J: Yeah, I can see how it all might seem perfectly ridiculous, but as the 'good book' says, "The love of God passes all understanding."

PJ: It certainly passes mine. Well, Jesus, thanks again for coming to the studio and giving us all an insight into the rum workings of the divine mind. Jesus Christ, ladies and gentlemen.

[Fade out to the hymn 'Jesus loves the little children.' (Sung by children).]

Matthew. 21: 18 – 32 and Mark. 11: 12 – 24

The Deadwood Sage

PJ: Ladies and gentlemen, I'm sure you'll agree it's a big thrill to have Jesus in the studio and talk to him about his unique career as saviour of the world. So, will you please give a big welcome to our boy from Nazareth, Jesus Christ.

(Enthusiastic applause as Jesus comes on stage, shakes Peremy's hand, and sits down. Walk-on music is 'I don't like Mondays' by The Boomtown Rats.)

PJ: Welcome to the show, Jesus; but before we get started, I should say that tonight's show is brought to you by the makers of Jacob's Fig Rolls, Jesus's favourite breakfast snack.

J: That's right. If they're good enough for God, they're good enough for you.

(Nibbling a fig roll he's taken from the plate) … mmm, lovely.

PJ: Jesus, I'd like to begin by asking you about the time you took the day off from your Messiah job.

J: That didn't happen. Saving the world is a 24/7 gig.

PJ: That's what I thought, but on the morning I have in mind, it looks like you rang heaven and called in sick.

J: What morning's that?

PJ: The morning after Palm Sunday, when you killed a tree for no reason.

J: Ah yes, that one. But I did have a reason. I was feeling hungry, and as I was walking along, I saw this fig tree up ahead, so I went up to it to get some figs for breakfast, but it didn't have any.

PJ: And since it didn't have any figs for you, you didn't give a fig for it, so you killed it on the spot.

J: It was barren anyway, and besides, from a distance it made a big show of having loads of figs, what with all those leaves, but when you got up close there weren't any.

PJ: So, you're telling me that you executed a tree because it was a hypocrite!? Isn't that just a little bit, you know… nuts? You're treating it as if it's responsible for its actions — as if it has free will.

J: But doesn't it have tree will?

PJ: Ha ha. No, there's no such thing. Tree will and free will are not the same.

J: They *sound* the same.

PJ: That's very sweet. I can see why people like you – but you can't hitch a ride on a rhyme and hope to reach the real. You know, people are starting to think you weren't playing with a full deck.

J: I'm fine.

PJ: You mugged a tree.

J: I just didn't want other people being fooled like I was, so I killed the tree to benefit humanity.

PJ: By 'humanity' you presumably mean a few stray people travelling that way, and by 'benefit' you mean saving them a few seconds' fruitless search for figs.

J: Every little helps.

PJ: Hey, you're a Tesco man!

J: No, I'm the Son of Man.

PJ: That's super. But the thing is, the help is so small it's pointless. I mean, the morning begins with a hungry Messiah and a fig tree and ends with an even *hungrier* Messiah and a *dead* fig tree. It's not what you'd call progress, is it? Most sane people would have done things differently.

J: Done things differently… how do you mean?

PJ: Well, I'm no Messiah, but if I'd been in your shoes, instead of killing the poor old tree, I'd have told it to produce figs on the spot. It's win, win. I'd no longer be hungry, and the tree would still be alive, and full of figs for everyone. Now that's what I call progress! Why didn't you think of something as obvious as that?

J: Because I wasn't trying to make that sort of progress. I was trying to send a message.

PJ: Oh, I think the tree got the message all right!

J: No, a message to humanity.

PJ: I think we've all got the message.

J: You have? That's great. So, what's the message?

PJ: "Hand over the goods or I'll kill you."

J: No, no, it's—

PJ: Don't tell me, don't tell me; is it, "Your figs or your life"?

J: No…

PJ: You know, you should meet Dick Turpin; he's a big fan.

J: You've got the message all wrong…

PJ: Well, can you tell us your message a bit later, if that's okay? What I'm interested in right now is what method you used to kill the tree.

J: Oh, that was easy. I just talked to it.

PJ: (Deadpan) You talked to a tree. The conversation must have been rather one-sided. Didn't the tree get to explain its side of the story?

J: No. I killed it before it had a chance to reply.

PJ: Shoot first and ask questions later, eh? You should meet Jesse James; he's a big fan... so, what did you say to it?

J: I cursed it.

PJ: I can imagine how *that* went: "Son of a bitch! No fucking figs! Call yourself a fig tree!?"

J: No, no. It wasn't that sort of cursing.

PJ: Ah, you mean it was more like an old-fashioned witch's curse?

J: Sort of.

PJ: What did you say?

J: Sort of.

PJ: No, I mean, to the tree.

J: I said, "May no fruit ever come from you again!"

PJ: And when the tree heard that, it died?

J: Yeah! Impressive isn't it?

PJ: The power is; the wording's not.

J: What's wrong with the wording?

PJ: You left a big loophole. If that tree had had a fancy lawyer, he could have explained to the tree that it could comply with your command without having to die. After all, it was already producing no fruit, so all it had to do was to continue to produce no fruit and, as you said, no fruit would ever come from it again. Your curse wouldn't have changed a thing.

J: I see your point. I guess I need to work on the wording of my curses.

PJ: Might I suggest, "Die you figless bastard!"

J: That's certainly less ambiguous. No loopholes there. I'll think about it.

PJ: Now Jesus, so far, we've been following Matthew's account of the fig tree debacle—

J: *Incident* — fig tree *incident*.

PJ: Sorry; fig tree *incident*. But fascinating though Matthew's account is, I'd like to move on to Mark's version in the hope that it will throw more light on what happened.

J: You know, they call me "The Light of the World."

PJ: You don't say! Well then, you're the very man we need to enlighten us.

J: I'll do all I can to help.

PJ: That's great. Can you begin by explaining why Mark says the fig tree didn't die till the following morning?

J: Er, can you run that one by me again, Peremy?

PJ: Yes of course; Matthew says the fig tree died immediately, but Mark says it held out for another day and died the next morning. Do you see a slight problem here?

J: I think so. We can't say that one of the accounts is wrong because the Holy Ghost wrote both of them and he'll never admit he's wrong — remember the murdered kids?

PJ: How could I forget?

J: So, if both accounts are true that can only mean one thing—

PJ: There were *two* trees!!

J: Exactly!

PJ: Well, that certainly solves that problem, but it doesn't do much for your image.

J: In what way?

PJ: Well, if you'd killed just one tree it could be seen as just a one-off tantrum but killing two in a row on the same morning looks more like the start of a rampage. You're not so much a 'gentle Jesus' — you're more a 'Christ that kicks ass'.

J: It looks bad, doesn't it?

PJ: Yes, but maybe you can turn the bad publicity to your advantage.

J: How?

PJ: Well, as you know, the church is steadily losing ground. It looks out of date and out of touch with today's teenagers.

J: Yes, I've been concerned about this for some time now. So how do we win the cool kids back?

PJ: You could start by juicing up Holy Week.

J: I beg your pardon.

PJ: You know… sexing it up a bit. Look, today's youngsters have been brought up on Zombies, Grand Theft Auto, and Red Dead Redemption. They need something more exciting than boring 'Palm Sunday', 'Good Friday', and 'Easter Sunday'.

J: You mean the church needs a raunchy rebranding of Holy Week?

PJ: Now you're talking. We could make a start with that Monday you zapped those trees.

J: What do you have in mind?

PJ: Well, let's see… we could re-name it, "Psycho tree-killer Day!"

J: (Doubtfully). A bit over the top; I'll think about it. What shall we call Palm Sunday?

PJ: That's the day you rode into Jerusalem on an ass and got a big welcome.

Mmmm… let's go with "Ass-riding Sunday"!

J: But won't people get the wrong idea?

PJ: Trust me; they need only recall the spare-time activities of Catholic priests, and believe you me, they'll get exactly the right idea!

J: I'm not sure that's the sort of idea I want them to get… anyway, let's move on to Good Friday. I've always hated that name. I mean, that's the day they crucified me. What the hell's good about that?

PJ: I see your point… how about, "The buggers nailed me up Day"?

J: (Still on his own train of thought) … I mean, if any day should be called 'good' it's Easter Sunday—that's the day I rose from the dead. We could re-name it "Good Sunday".

PJ: You're on the right track, but it's still a bit understated. I mean, ice cream is good, but the Son of God conquering death and saving the world has got to be better than ice cream!

J: You're right. We can't have people comparing the Resurrection to a banana split.

PJ: Exactly. Death couldn't hold you; you shot out of that grave like a bungee jump in reverse… I've got it! We'll call it "Zoom Tomb Sunday"!!

J: Great. That's the lot. "Ass-riding Sunday", "Psycho-tree-killer day", "'The buggers nailed me up day", ending with "Zoom Tomb Sunday".

PJ: Not quite. I think we need a name for the Thursday—that's the day Judas betrayed you.

J: Yeah. That bloody hurt! He had the nerve to betray me with a kiss.

PJ: Yes, it's called irony.

J: No, it's called taking the piss.

PJ: You've forgiven him of course. It's what you do.

J: Yes, I'm over it now. Forgive and forget; that's my motto.

PJ: So, what do you think we should call Thursday?

J: (With feeling). "Back-stabbing Bastard Day!"

PJ: That's the spirit! The kids'll be flocking to the churches in no time.

J: I should contact some influential church leaders to get the ball rolling. I'll ring the Pope after the interview.

PJ: What about the Archbishop of Canterbury?

J: I said, '*influential*'.

PJ: You're right. What was I thinking? Now let's get back to those two dead fig trees. How did you kill the second one?

J: Same way I killed the first.

PJ: You cursed it? I can imagine how *that* went. "Son of a bitch! No fuck…"

J: Let's not go through that again. It was the other kind of curse.

PJ: What did you say to it?

J: I said, "May no one ever eat fruit from you again."

PJ: You see… there you go again with your loopholes. If that second tree had hired a top-class lawyer, he'd have pointed out that his client could comply with your command without having to die. After all, it was already true that no one was eating fruit from it due to its lack of fruit, and all it had to do was continue to lack fruit and, as you said, no one would ever have eaten fruit from it again. So, this second curse wouldn't have changed a thing either.

J: Yeah, you're right. I really need to hire a good lawyer to help me with my curses.

PJ: Well, you'd better hire one quick.

J: Why?

PJ: Because of this: (hands Jesus a bible open at Mark 11). Would you be so kind as to read Mark's gospel chapter 11 verses 12 and 13?

J: (Jesus reads): *"On the following day, when they came from Bethany, he was hungry. Seeing in the distance a fig tree in leaf, he went to see whether perhaps he would find anything on it. When he came to it, he found nothing but leaves, for it was not the season for figs."* (Stunned, he reads the last line again) *"**for it was not the season for figs.**"*

PJ: That's right. 'It was not the season for figs'. You know what that means?

J: It means they weren't barren at all. It means I killed two perfectly healthy fig trees!

PJ: It also means you didn't have a clue what season of the year it was despite living all your life there.

J: I know it looks bad but—

PJ: You realise you've alienated the entire Green lobby. You see, what you did wasn't exactly environmentally friendly. They claim you've given the green light to wholesale deforestation.

J: But it was only two trees, not a whole forest.

PJ: True, but it's the *principle* of the thing. The guys stripping the rainforest argue that killing healthy trees must be okay because Jesus did it. You should arrange a business lunch with some Amazonian Logging companies; they're big fans.

J: But this is terrible!

PJ: Yeah. They've got you pegged as one bad-ass logger.

J: But I only logged two trees.

PJ: Apparently, it's not so much the *numbers* they admire, but rather your *whole approach* to logging. *That's* what they're in awe of.

J: My whole approach? What are you talking about?

PJ: Well, for a start, you don't need all that expensive machinery. Just a few words from you and trees fall like ninepins. And what's more, you don't even make use of the wood afterwards. You just leave the trees to rot. That's logging with attitude! But what really impresses them is that, unlike them, you treat logging as a personal vendetta against trees that have pissed you off. Frankly, they feel like wusses in comparison.

J: But this is awful!

PJ: Look on the bright side; lumberjacks have voted you 'pin-up boy of the year'!

J: Wow! That's the second time I've won that award.

PJ: You don't say. When was the first time?

J: Oh, about 2000 years ago. The Jews voted me their pin-up boy of the year — *and meant it*... Anyway, the main point in killing the fig trees was not to impress lumberjacks, but to teach a message to my disciples.

PJ: Ah yes. This is the message you wanted to talk about earlier. It should explain the whole thing, shouldn't it?

J: Yes. You see I used the example of the dead fig trees to teach my disciples that if they had enough faith, they could also kill trees, and what's more, they could throw mountains into the sea by just telling them to shift. All they have to do is simply believe that what they say will come true, and it will.

PJ: That's an absolutely amazing message! No wonder you've been called the greatest teacher ever. The thing is though, do we really want millions of Christians killing trees and moving mountains around on a daily basis? It'll play havoc with geography.

J: You worry too much. That sort of thing doesn't happen a lot.

PJ: Maybe you could tell us just how often it *has* happened. For instance, how many of your 12 disciples actually killed a tree or moved a mountain?

J: Er… none.

PJ: And how many Christians over the past 2000 years have talked a tree to death and told a mountain to clear off?

J: Er… none.

PJ: So, you're saying that if there was a GCSE in tree-killing and mountain-moving, every single one of your pupils in a class of billions would have failed it?

J: Er… yes.

PJ: You'll perhaps understand why many observers think the whole thing was an exercise in utter futility. What do you say to the growing number of critics who think you're certifiable?

J: I'd say they think this because they don't see with the eyes of faith.

PJ: And you do of course.

J: Of course.

PJ: Could you explain why your eyes of faith failed to inform you what time of year it was and didn't happen to notice that it wasn't the season for figs?

J: I know it looks bad but—

PJ: It's about to look a whole lot worse.

J: How could it be any worse?

PJ: Apparently none of your 12 disciples noticed it either, otherwise they would have had a quiet word in your ear before you made a complete fool of yourself.

J: I'm not a fool; I'm a sage.

PJ: (Reassuring and condescending — putting his hand on Jesus's arm) Of *course* you are! But how come those disciples of yours didn't know what season it was?

J: I can see there's a problem. I can't explain their stupidity by claiming that they used the eyes of faith rather than their normal eyes, because, well, they all failed their faith GCSE.

PJ: Well, this might help; critics are divided between two theories. The first theory is that you picked a bunch of idiots. The second theory is that they were smoking some serious shit the night before.

J: The first theory looks more likely; they had the best teacher in the world and they still all failed. It couldn't have been my fault.

PJ: The sentiments of millions of teachers worldwide. Everyone knows that a teacher with a 100% failure rate deserves nothing but praise.

J: What's the evidence for the second theory?

PJ: Well, for a start, they all stayed up late the night before.

J: On Palm Sunday.

PJ: Yes.

J: But staying up late isn't much to go on.

PJ: Not on its own, but whatever it was they were doing, the next morning they were so spaced out none of them knew whether it was summer or winter, and what's more, a couple of days later they couldn't even stay awake when you were praying in Gethsemane.

J: What are you trying to say?

PJ: Surely you don't think that palm leaves were the only leaves they were waving around?

J: You mean some other kind of leaf may have been involved?

PJ: Jesus, wake up and smell the ganja!

J: Oh my God! People are going to start calling it "Spliff Sunday!" How on earth do I explain all this to my heavenly Father?

PJ: You mean "Big Daddio?"

J: (Urgently and in a loud whisper) Shhh! This is not the time. He might hear you!

PJ: Take it easy. He'll mellow when he sees the churches packed with all those chilled-out worshippers. But maybe we'd better talk about something else to round off the interview. Let's go on a journey of discovery.

J: I don't do drugs.

PJ: No. Not that kind of journey.

J: Great! I love adventures.

PJ: Okay. What do you think was the origin of Christianity?

J: That's a biggy, but it's dead easy... ME.

PJ: And what happened to you that sparked things off?

J: I was crucified by the Jews and Romans and rose from the dead. You know, so far this journey is a bit of a drag. I haven't discovered anything yet.

PJ: Don't worry, you soon will. Now, what happened to Guy Fawkes when he tried to wreck the Houses of Parliament?

J: That's a bit of a leap... mmm, he was executed. Politicians don't muck about when you hit them where it hurts.

PJ: Quite right. And what did you do just a few days before they executed you?

J: I started a one-man riot in the Temple on Psycho tree-killer day. I went bananas and wrecked the joint because they'd turned it into a marketplace instead of a place of worship.

PJ: But the Temple was used for something else too.

J: That's right. It was the centre of power for the Jews and Romans. It doubled as their 'Houses of Parliament'. Are you saying there's a connection between me and Guy Fawkes?

PJ: Yes.

J: This is getting interesting. Go on!

PJ: So, when you cleared the Temple out, they saw it as a revolutionary act of insurrection and plotted to kill you.

J: Just like Guy Fawkes! So, the Temple incident led directly to the crucifixion less than a week later.

PJ: Precisely. Now, here's the really interesting bit; you didn't just go bananas when you saw the state of the Temple; your brain was *already* in the banana zone earlier that morning when you were transformed from gentle Jesus to a fig-craving, tree-killing maniac.

J: It looks really bad doesn't it?

PJ: It's okay. That's what constipation does to people.

J: What!? You think I was constipated!?

PJ: It all fits. You're angry, frustrated, violent, and irrational; you're on the hunt for *figs,* of all things. Why *figs* in *particular*? There must have been all sorts of trees around yet nothing but *figs* would do you... and I think you know why.

J: Mmm... I was in dire need of a laxative, and figs are the rock stars of the laxative world!?

PJ: And now you know the *real* origin of Christianity.

J: (The penny drops). (Thoughtfully going over the sequence of events) ... Constipation was behind my angry search for figs; the exact same anger which later that very day caused the Temple riot, which caused the crucifixion which caused Christianity... Oh my God! Constipation is the origin of Christianity!

PJ: That's right. As Americans might say, 'No crucifixion without constipation.' And on that bombshell, ladies and gentlemen, we must end the show. Please give a big round of applause to our special guest, Jesus Christ.

(Fade out to Doris Day singing 'The Deadwood Stage' from 'Calamity Jane', as a Jesus, still in shock, shuffles his way off stage.)

Matthew. 14: 21 – 34, Mark. 6: 44 – 53, John. 6: 16 – 21, Luke. 9: 10 – 17

God's Boy Ahoy!

(The 'Sailor's Hornpipe' plays as Peremy comes on stage)

PJ: Good evening ladies and gentlemen. Our next interview with Jesus will have a nautical flavour as our Lord has kindly agreed to talk about the time he walked on water across the Sea of Galilee. So, without further ado, please will you give it up for everyone's favourite old salt, Jesus Christ!

(Jesus comes on to applause — background music is 'We're riding along on the crest of a wave' [the Scouts' Anthem])

PJ: (Welcoming him and shaking his hand). Well hello sailor! Welcome aboard the show. (Gestures to the clapping audience) — see how popular you are!? I bet you have a disciple in every port.

J: Thanks, Peremy; it's a pleasure to be on deck.

PJ: First of all, I'd like to congratulate you on coming up with what is quite possibly *the* definitive miracle. When people are asked for an example of the miraculous, probably the first thing they think of is 'walking on water'.

J: You're too kind, but yes, you're right. You see, if you want what you do to be remembered, it needs to be a one-off and possess a uniqueness all its own. When I walked on the water, I was going for what the IRA used to call "a spectacular", so I only did it the once.

PJ: Couldn't you have healed a leper instead?

J: I suppose so, but where I come from, lepers are 10-a-penny and healing *them* just doesn't have the same cachet.

PJ: True, true, and that's why we can't wait to hear what you have to tell us about this spectacular miracle. I mean, all we know is that it happened somewhere on the Sea of Galilee. It would be nice if we had a more specific location.

J: Well, I'll do all I can to help. Where do you want me to start?

PJ: Maybe you could start by filling us in on the background to the miracle. What was the setting?

J: Well, it was just after I'd finished feeding the 5000 with the loaves and fishes. I remember it was beginning to get dark, around 7 or 8 in the evening, so I made the disciples get into the boat and go across to Capernaum on the other side of the lake while I dismissed the crowd. After the crowd had dispersed, I went up into the hills to pray, and when I came back to the shore, I saw the disciples having a hard time of it rowing against an almost gale-force wind. The waves were beating against the boat, and that's when I decided to walk to them on the water.

PJ: That's a wonderful summary. If you don't mind, I'd like to use a map of the Sea of Galilee to help make things even clearer for our audience.

J: Knock yourself out.

PJ: (Gets out a large map of the Sea of Galilee and gives a brief outline of its main features).

(To the audience). As you can see, the Sea of Galilee is actually a lake, eight miles wide at its widest point, and thirteen miles long, with the cities of Capernaum and Gennesaret on its north-western shore, and the city of Bethsaida at its most northerly point.

(To Jesus). Now if, as you say, you sent your disciples to Capernaum on the other side of the lake from where you fed the 5000, you must have been somewhere on the north-east side of the lake when you sent them off in the boat. (Gestures to the map).

J: Yeah, that makes sense.

PJ: But there's a problem with that.

J: Already? But I haven't even started walking on the water yet.

PJ: The problem's not about that. It's about what your disciples were up to.

J: Not them again. What did they do this time?

PJ: Well, although according to John's gospel they set off for Capernaum like you wanted, according to Matthew's gospel they actually landed at Gennesaret three miles down the coast. How did they manage to be as much as three miles out on a five-mile trip?

J: Maybe the wind blew them off course.

PJ: No, it can't be that. It would have had to be blowing from the north against the right side of the boat. But it says in the gospels that they were rowing *against* the wind, so it must have been blowing from the west—the direction they were rowing in. All it would do is slow them down.

J: I see. Then maybe they lost their bearings.

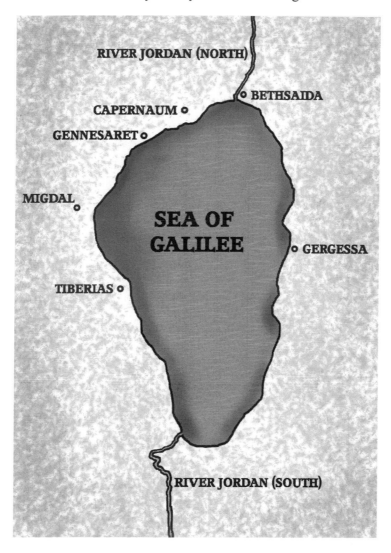

PJ: You mean… they got lost.

J: Er… yes.

PJ: (Incredulous). On a five-mile boat ride?

J: Well, the sea can sometimes play funny tricks on you.

PJ: It's not the middle of the Atlantic. It's a 13 by 8 lake. They've fished that lake all their lives, so they should know it like the back of their hand. Do you think they'd had a skinful?

J: How'd they get hold of drink in the middle of a lake?

PJ: Are you sure you didn't turn the water into wine before you walked on it?

J: Of course not. And anyway, it would read funny in the gospels, "And he came towards them walking on the wine."

PJ: I see. So, the best explanation is that they were simply incompetent sailors.

J: Well, you don't have to have a high IQ to be one of my disciples.

PJ: It seems you don't even need an average one.

J: What makes you say that?

PJ: Because on top of being lost, they didn't even *realise* they were lost!

J: How do you know that?

PJ: Because when they landed at Gennesaret instead of Capernaum nobody said, "Hey guys, guess what? We've landed in the wrong town!"

J: Well, when you've seen one of these Galilean towns you've seen them all.

PJ: Are you actually saying that when they were in Gennesaret they thought they were in Capernaum?

J: Don't you think it's *just* possible?

PJ: With those idiots!? Actually... yes... Okay, now I'd like to move on to Mark's account of what happened, if that's all right?

J: Please do. All the gospel accounts are inspired by the Holy Ghost so it should be pretty straightforward.

PJ: Wonderful. It's a great relief to have the reliable Holy Ghost there when we need him. So, since it's pretty straightforward, maybe you could give us a straightforward explanation of why you sent the disciples off in the boat to Bethsaida instead of Capernaum. (Gestures to Bethsaida on the map).

J: What!?

PJ: Yes. Mark's gospel says you sent them across to Bethsaida on the other side of the lake. He doesn't even mention Capernaum.

J: But since they're aiming for the other side, and Bethsaida's at the north end, that means I must have been somewhere on the south shore, not the north–east shore. (Gestures to the map).

PJ: Correct.

J: Mmm… it's not quite as straightforward as I thought. At least tell me they landed at Bethsaida.

PJ: Sorry. I'm afraid we're back in their favourite town.

J: They landed at Gennesaret again!?

PJ: I'm afraid so. It seems no matter where you send them they always end up in Gennesaret. What's the big attraction?

J: Beats me.

PJ: Do you think it's women?

J: Why women?

PJ: Because *normal* sailors have a girl in every port. These aren't normal sailors, so maybe they have all their girls in the one port—

PJ and J: (In unison). Gennesaret!

J: Mmm… it's a thought, but maybe them not being normal means they don't have any girls in any ports. My money's on them being lost again.

PJ: Knowing them, that's probably it. But Gennesaret is about eight miles from Bethsaida. How on earth did they manage to be eight miles out, on a thirteen-mile trip?

J: The same way they managed to be three miles out, on a five-mile trip.

PJ: They must have sucked at fishing. And did you notice that the error ratios match? 3/5 is almost identical to 8/13.

J: Yeah, well at least they sucked consistently.

PJ: That's a comfort.

J: No wonder they jumped at the chance to be my disciples. That lot had trouble finding the shore never mind the fish.

PJ: You'd think they'd be grateful, but no. In your hour of need they all deserted you.

J: Oh, I wouldn't be too hard on them. They probably got lost in downtown Jerusalem and couldn't find Golgotha!

(They both laugh).

PJ: But Jesus, you still haven't explained how you can send them to Bethsaida and Capernaum at the same time.

J: Well, I must have meant to send them to Bethsaida *by way of* Capernaum.

PJ: I see. That would be a great solution to the problem… except for one thing.

J: What's that?

PJ: Luke's gospel says you fed the 5000 in Bethsaida. You see the problem?

J: What problem?

PJ: Well, you see, you sent them off in the boat just after you fed the 5000. Now, if you fed the 5000 in Bethsaida...

J: (The problem dawning on him) ... it means they're *already* in Bethsaida with me! Then how on earth can I send them off in the boat across the lake to Bethsaida when they're already in it!?

PJ: Exactly! It would set the world record for the shortest boat trip ever.

J: Even *they* couldn't possibly get lost on a trip like that!

PJ: Don't bet on it.

J: It looks bad doesn't it? This is a right mess!

PJ: Well, you know who wrote all this stuff and got you into this mess.

J: The Holy Ghost. Maybe I should have a word with him about all this.

PJ: While you're at it you can tell him from me that he sucks at geography.

J: Oh, he won't like that. Knowing him, he'll probably come after you, and when he finds you, you'll be in big trouble.

PJ: Finds me!? With *his* sense of direction? He can't even find his way round a 13 by 8 lake. He should be called "The Wholly Lost", not "The Holy Ghost."

J: I see your point. Maybe I should try and sort this mess out myself. Let me see... (Thinks)... I know—what if there were *two* Bethsaidas, and I was sending them from the one to the other?

PJ: So, since you're already in Bethsaida at the north end of the lake, Bethsaida number two would be down here somewhere. (Gestures to the south coast).

J: Yes.

PJ: If only that were true, but there isn't a shred of evidence for a second Bethsaida. Archaeologists have been digging till they're blue in the face, but they've found nothing, so I'm afraid that while doubling up on trees may have helped with the fig tree debacle...

J: *Incident... fig tree incident...*

PJ: Doubling up on Bethsaidas won't help you here.

J: I see... mmm... er...

PJ: Okay, while you're thinking it over, let me just summarise for our audience where we've got to so far.

(To audience and using the map).

We began with the knowledge that Jesus here, walked on water *somewhere* on the Sea of Galilee (Gestures to the lake as a whole). But now we know, thanks to consulting the Holy Ghost, that he either walked from around here (Gestures to the north-east coast) to here (Points to 'Capernaum') or here (Points to Gennesaret), or walked from somewhere around here (Gestures towards the south coast), to here (Points to Bethsaida) or here (Points to Gennesaret), or walked from here (Points to Bethsaida) to an imaginary Bethsaida somewhere around here (Gestures to the south coast).

In short, we now know that Jesus walked on water *somewhere* on the Sea of Galilee (Gestures to the lake as a whole), and I'm sure you'll all agree that the Holy Ghost has been a big help in advancing our knowledge, and I for one expected no less.

(Turning to Jesus). Now then Lord, have you made any more progress than we have?

J: You know, the best sense I can make of sending them from Bethsaida to Bethsaida, is that I sent them out in the boat from Bethsaida to row to the other side of the lake, and then come straight back to Bethsaida.

PJ: Are you insane!? That's a twenty-six-mile round trip. What's the point in sending them to row thirteen miles to nowhere — look, there's nothing there, (Pointing to the south of the lake) — only to row thirteen miles back to where they started, *and* do it in the middle of the night!?

J: But there's method in my madness, because I did it to get rid of them for several hours while I got peace to pray to my heavenly Father up in the hills.

PJ: But couldn't you have just told them to hang out on the beach while you prayed? Why all the rowing?

J: Because then I wouldn't have had an excuse to walk on the sea. If they're on the beach while I'm walking about offshore, I'd just be showboating, and that's bad for my image. I needed them to be in the boat on the water so I could walk *to* them on the sea.

PJ: But then walking on the water would amount to no more than a convenient short cut across the lake because you couldn't be bothered to take the long way round on land. That's bad for your image too.

J: That's why we needed the storm.

PJ: I beg your pardon!?

J: Don't you see? The disciples need to be in trouble in the middle of the sea, battling against a near gale-force wind, waves beating against the boat. That way, it's no longer a short cut, but a rescue mission instead.

PJ: Are you saying that the storm was rigged just so you could look good walking on the water to rescue them?

J: Clever, eh?

PJ: Yes, but not clever enough.

J: In what way?

PJ: Well, for a start, you took your own sweet time about it. All the accounts say you came walking towards them in the 4th watch of the night. That's somewhere between 3.00 a.m. and 6.00 a.m. That means they'd been out there in the storm for around seven hours before you even set off! It's not exactly an emergency service you're running there.

J: What are you trying to say?

PJ: I'm saying that if you were a firefighter, you'd be fired.

J: But I was praying.

PJ: I'm afraid that doesn't wash with the public these days. People take a very dim view of firefighters who don't respond to emergency calls because they're too busy praying.

J: I see. Anything else?

PJ: Yes, if you were *really* keen to rescue your disciples why didn't you go faster than walking pace? You basically *strolled* to the rescue, when you should have been sprinting.

J: But walking is so much more dignified. If the gospels had said, "And Jesus came to them sprinting on the sea", they'd have made me look ridiculous. That's one reason I didn't do cartwheels.

PJ: Are you saying your image is more important than your disciples' lives?

J: It's okay; I knew they'd be safe. It was all in the plan.

PJ: Yeah, but *they* didn't know that.

J: What can I say? It's all part of the human condition.

PJ: Yeah, and we all know who's responsible for that. Thanks a lot.

J: You're welcome.

PJ: Okay, so the disciples are about four miles out to sea—how did you know they were having trouble rowing against the wind?

J: I could see them from the shore.

PJ: Wow! How could you see a small boat tossed on the sea that far away? It was a whole four miles, and on top of that, it must have been pitch black!

J: My eyeballs are miraculously turbocharged.

PJ: It's funny how your turbo-vision can spot a tiny boat four miles away in the dark but can't see there's no figs on a tree fifty yards away in broad daylight.

J: Yeah, that *is* funny.

PJ: Okay, let's get back to the disciples. From the shore you can see that they're having a hard time, so off you go walking towards them on the water. How'd you do it? Did you wear special cruise shoes?

J: No. The miracle lies in the feet. I have anti-gravity feet, and they need to be seaworthy—no holes.

PJ: Ahh… *that's* why you didn't try this after you'd been crucified—you'd have sprung a leak!

J: Two leaks, actually.

PJ: Of course. Now, with that rough sea bucking and tossing you around, you must have looked like a rodeo cowboy out there.

J: A bit; but I've ridden enough donkeys in my time — I was almost born on one! — so I was able to cope. But the waves were a bit of a problem.

PJ: How's that?

J: Well, they were coming at me between four and five feet high, so I had to clamber over them and sort of surf down the other side. I call it "Galilean water-skiin'".

PJ: So, you came to them clambering, rodeo riding, and surfing on the water.

J: "Walking" sounds so much better.

PJ: Ah yes — the image. Now, when you finally reached them you got into the boat and that was the cue for the wind to stop.

J: Yes.

PJ: Can you explain to your critics why you didn't stop the wind as soon as you'd seen their plight from the shore? It would have been a lot sooner and saved them a lot of trouble.

J: That's true, but then they wouldn't have known it was *me* who did it.

PJ: So, it's not enough to perform the miracle; you must also get the credit for it even if it means prolonging the agony?

J: Well, it's not as if they were actually sinking. They were just finding it heavy going.

PJ: Which makes a lot of people wonder why you went to all that trouble for just twelve guys who weren't actually in mortal danger, when you didn't even lift a finger to save the Titanic.

J: Good question; but I was busy sitting at the right hand of God the Father, so you'll need to take the matter up with him.

PJ: A lot of people already have, but his reply wasn't satisfactory.

J: Why not?

PJ: Because there was no reply. Anyway, leaving that aside, I'd like to ask you about an amazing thing that happened when you got into the boat. John's gospel says that you were all *immediately* at the shore. Now that's super-fast. I was wondering whether you miraculously engaged warp speed or beamed everyone to the beach instead.

J: The name's Jesus H. Christ, not James T. Kirk.

PJ: Sorry, I just thought that since you were the inspiration for 'Star Trek' that...

J: *Me!?...* inspire 'Star Trek'?

PJ: You know, with the Wise Men using the star to trek all that way to... oh never mind. Let's leave that for now. What I'm interested in is what you did when you reached your disciples — you actually got into the boat. Perhaps you could explain why you bothered doing that.

J: Why is that puzzling? People get into boats all the time.

PJ: Yes, but none of *them* can walk on water. Do you see the problem? It's like finding Superman sitting next to you on your Ryanair flight. I mean, why is he even there?

J: Ah, *I* get it. Like Spiderman using a stepladder to paint the ceiling.

PJ: Precisely!

J: I don't know really... I suppose I thought it would be more of a comfort for them to have me in the boat with them.

PJ: Of course, but it's a pity you didn't think of their comfort earlier when you scared the bejesus out of them. They thought you were a ghost coming to them on the water!

J: Yes, but at least I helped them in the end. So, you see, walking on the water *was* a successful rescue mission.

PJ: Except it was nothing of the sort.

J: Eh!?

PJ: Can you read what the Holy Ghost has to say in Mark's gospel chapter 6 verses 47 and 48?

J: (Reading). *"When evening came, the boat was out on the lake, and he was alone on the land. When he saw that they were straining at the oars, against an adverse wind, he came towards them early in the morning, walking on the lake. He intended to pass them by. But when they saw him…"* (Reads the crucial line again) … ***He intended to pass them by.*** (Stops reading and looks shocked).

J: *That* doesn't sound good.

PJ: You see the problem?

J: Yes. It can't have been a rescue mission if I simply intended to walk on by and just leave them to it.

PJ: Yeah; it looks like you were only interested in number one. As miracles go, it's what we'd call a "Selfie". We're back to the short cut theory, for why else would you walk past them without helping unless you were solely intent on getting to the other side by the shortest route possible? You come across as a callous bastard who didn't give a damn about them.

J: I know it looks bad but—

PJ: You do realise you've ended up on the wrong end of your famous "Good Samaritan" parable? You'll never guess what they're calling you.

J: What?

PJ: The Bad Samaritime.

J: Oh my God! It's really bad isn't it? If only there was another explanation that makes me look good.

PJ: Well Jesus, you're in luck.

J: You mean you've thought of something!?

PJ: Yes.

J: What is it?

PJ: You won't like it.

J: Just tell me what it is!

PJ: You won't look great, but you will look better…

J: (Desperate by now). ***For Christ's sake, spill it!***

PJ: Okay, okay… Here goes… *The whole thing was a huge practical joke!*

J: Are you crazy!? What will people think of me pulling a stunt like that!?

PJ: I told you, you wouldn't like it.

J: Who ever heard of a prankster Messiah busy doing miracles just so he can amuse himself by scaring the shit out of his own disciples!?

PJ: Will you just hear me out? It's not as bad as it sounds.

J: Okay, but this better be good!

PJ: If we go with the line that the whole thing was a set-up, everything magically falls into place. First of all, you send them off all unsuspecting in the boat, and spin them a yarn about how you need to stay behind so you can have some time for private prayer. Who wouldn't buy a story like that coming from you? Next, you delay for several hours, letting them stew in the boat out in the middle of the sea; and then you throw in a storm for good measure. That gives you the perfect background atmospherics: it's dark, the wind's howling, waves crashing against the boat; they're sleepy, tired, on edge. Then you wait till the most godforsaken hour of the night before you walk hauntingly across the waves in your all-white Casper outfit. (Let's face it, that robe is as good as a bedsheet). You make as if to go past them, and you're just about to yell, "I'm off to kill your mothers!" when they see you and go nuts, screaming and shouting, "It's a ghost!! It's a ghost!!" I can picture the absolute panic in the boat. There's nowhere to run from the apparition. What a hoot! You've invented the horror movie and the practical joke in one go right there! It's sheer genius.

J: Okay… I can see some merit in your explanation, but doesn't the fact that these are my own disciples count against it?

PJ: Actually, it's quite the opposite, given the sort of men your disciples were. These are fishermen who can't fish; sailors who keep getting lost in a lake; hangers-on who are only there for the free hand-outs of wine, bread and fish (God knows, they can't catch any on their own); and who, when the chips are down, betray you, deny you, and finally desert you. In short, they're a bunch of wankers, and if anyone ever deserved to have the crap scared out of them, it's them!

J: You think then that people will see the funny side of this?

PJ: Of course. Look, there isn't a single laugh in the whole New Testament. Readers will be delighted to find you have a lighter side to your nature. "JESUS — *Saviour, Healer, Joker.*"

J: Mmm… As you say, the joker part isn't great, but I'll take it, since the alternative is, *"Saviour, Healer, Callous Bastard"*.

PJ: That's more like it. You know, maybe you could branch out into other areas of comedy. Have you thought of doing 'Stand-Up'?

J: Well, there is a hymn that goes, "Stand up. Stand up for Jesus." But I never took its advice seriously. You think I'd be any good at one-liners?

PJ: Yeah; we could even be a double act. I could be the straight man. Let's give it a try. I'll ask you a question and you reply with a one-liner.

J: Okay.

PJ: Jesus, why did you decide to walk on the water?

J: Because I can't swim.

(Both laugh)

PJ: Jesus, what were you thinking on the cross?

J: I was thinking, "What a way to spend Easter."

PJ: Ha ha. You see? You're a natural.

J: You mean, a "*super*natural".

(Both laugh).

PJ: Jesus, thank you so much for being on the show. Ladies and gentlemen, I'm sure you'll agree it's been a pleasure having Jesus for our guest tonight, so please put your hands together to show your appreciation for the Messiah. Jesus Christ, ladies and gentlemen!

(Fade out with the theme from 'Ghostbusters').

Matthew. 8: 28 – 34; Mark. 5: 1 – 20; Luke. 8: 26 – 39

The Animal Rights Inactivist

(Applause, as Peremy comes on stage. Walk-on music is 'Summer Holiday', by Cliff Richard).

PJ: Good evening ladies and gentlemen. You'll be delighted to hear that the Son of God has once more agreed to be our special guest on the show tonight. So please give a big welcome to the meekest, mildest, man on the planet, Jesus Christ!

(Loud applause as Jesus walks on, waving and acknowledging the warm reception, and then sits down. Walk-on music is, 'Old Macdonald had a Farm' — the verse with the pig).

PJ: It's great to see you again, Jesus.

J: Right back at you, Peremy. I always look forward to our conversations for it gives me a chance to spread the word and answer any questions people might want to ask.

PJ: Marvellous! Well, it so happens that we took a poll of our studio audience, and there was only one question on everyone's lips.

J: What question was that, Peremy?

PJ: Why'd you kill all those pigs, Jesus?

J: Er... can you back up a minute there, Peremy? Would you like to fill me in on the details? A lot happened in that final year of my life, but I don't recall killing any pigs.

PJ: Yes, it *was* a sensational year; you couldn't move for miracles, but this miracle was one of the most sensational.

J: Well, a pig-killing miracle would definitely be sensational, but it doesn't sound like something I'd do. When did it happen?

PJ: It was when you were in the land of the Gadarenes — Gentile territory, east of the Sea of Galilee. You met a madman called Legion...

J: Ah, I remember now. The Gentiles called him Legion because he had so many demons. A sad case... he lived among the tombs. They'd tried to control him with chains, but he would tear the chains apart with his awesome strength, and he would often cry out in a strange voice.

PJ: Sounds like Arnie on a bad day.

J: Who?

PJ: So, what happened?

J: I had a chat with the demons and told them I wanted them out.

PJ: Amazing. How could you chat with thousands of demons at the same time?

J: They had a spokes-demon.

PJ: I see. And what did he say to you?

J: He begged me to let them enter the pigs in the nearby field instead of sending them back to hell.

PJ: They actually had the nerve to negotiate with you? I bet you didn't have to think twice: *"To hell with you, you henchmen of Satan!"* Eh?

J: Er... no, not quite.

PJ: What do you mean, "Not quite."? Don't tell me you actually did what they wanted?

J: Er... yes. And that's when the pigs all went charging down the hillside into the sea and were drowned. So, you see, I didn't kill the pigs; it was the demons.

PJ: Yes, the demons that were sent there by *you.* That'll play well in court. *"Oh, it wasn't me, your honour; it was the hitman I sent."*

J: Hey Peremy, that's not fair. When you send a hitman you intend to kill, and you can foresee the outcome. But when I sent the demons into the pigs, I didn't intend to kill them, and I certainly didn't think they'd all end up drowned in the Sea of Galilee.

PJ: All right, I'll grant you that. But you should know enough about demons to know it couldn't end well. Those pigs were happy and contented, feeding on the hillside. You can't seriously claim that you thought demons were just the thing to make their lives complete.

J: Well, in one sense the demons did complete their lives... ha ha... er... but that's probably not the sense you have in mind, is it? But you're right, demons and pigs are not a good mix.

PJ: Demons and *anything* is not a good mix. I mean, you saw what they did to Legion. He wasn't exactly living the dream, was he? So why did you make a decision you knew would destroy the happiness of 2000 innocent pigs?

J: Yeah, it looks bad. There were *2000* of them? Boy, I don't do things by halves, do I?

PJ: So why did you do it?

J: Well, I can't think of a single plausible motive at the minute.

PJ: There's something else.

J: What?

PJ: That very same decision makes it look like you're cosying up to Satan, because you're doing favours for his cronies. The gospels have you in cahoots with demons for goodness sake! What on earth were you thinking?

J: Okay, it looks *really* bad.

PJ: Yeah, and there's a nasty rumour going round, that the pigs were singing '*What a friend we have in Jesus*' as they plunged to their doom.

J: But this is just terrible! All those years I worked at being meek and mild are going down the drain.

PJ: Well, I suppose we could try and salvage something of your reputation. We need a motive that makes you look good... mmm, how about, 'Jesus loves everybody, and that includes demons'?

J: Me, love demons? Out of the question. Isn't it bad enough that I have to love... (swallows hard) ... American televangelists!?

PJ: Lord have mercy! Compared to them, even snakes walk tall.

J: (Ploughing on) ... Not to mention, estate agents, politicians, lawyers, and... (swallows even harder) ... second-hand car salesmen.

PJ: You call that having mercy!? I think I'm going to be sick.

J: Peremy, for Christ's sake, man up! Compared to loving that shower, crucifixion was a walk in the park, but if I can stand to *do* it, the least you can do is stand to *think* it.

PJ: You're right... okay, I'll try and soldier on... (with some effort) ... so, since we can't use the 'Jesus loves demons' excuse, what about, 'Jesus hates pigs'?

J: Too strong.

PJ: Okay, something weaker... I know! 'Jesus has pigophobia.'

J: That's better, but how did I become pigophobic?

PJ: Childhood trauma... a pig sat on your face in the manger and ever since then—

J: Definitely not! I can't appear unhinged.

PJ: Okay, so you're a hinged Messiah—a mental James Bond.

J: What?

PJ: I mean, mentally speaking, you're James Bond.

J: Who?

PJ: Samson with an on-side Delilah.

J: Got it. Hey, how about, 'Pigs aren't kosher, so it's all right to kill them'?

PJ: Two problems with that: 1) They're kosher for Gentiles. 2) They weren't your pigs to kill. The cops could get you for destruction of property. What would you think if a vegetarian fanatic sees a man eating a steak and suddenly decides to throw it in the fish tank?

J: I'm doomed. There's no motive that makes me look good.

PJ: Jesus, you're a genius.

J: I am?

PJ: Yes. You said it yourself, 'There's no motive.' We've been looking for good motives when there were none to be found. No wonder we were stumped.

J: But if there's no motive, then that would just make it a random decision. That's bad for my image.

PJ: Yeah, but it's not as bad as being a pig-hating, demon-lover.

J: Okay, let's call it a snap decision; but won't we need some explanation for *that*? I mean, what led to such a poor choice?

PJ: I don't know yet. I need some time to think it through.

J: Well, can you please be quick? There's someone who wants a word with me after the show, and I'll need a good story.

PJ: Who is it?

J: I can't pronounce their name; it's spelt funny.

PJ: How's it spelt?

J: R... S... P... C... A

PJ: I see... in that case, you're going to need a *very* good story. But don't worry; I'm sure I'll think of something. In the meantime, can we talk about the economic aftermath of your decision? Let's start with the swineherds.

J: What about them?

PJ: You've thrown them out of work. What are they going to live on now? They've no money to buy food or pay the rent.

J: I'm sure they could get another job.

PJ: With *that* on their CV? Yeah right. I can picture the interview:

"Come in and take a seat. Thanks for your interest in *'Swineherds a-go-go'*. I see you have... hey, aren't you the guy who was in charge of 2000 pigs when they went gallivanting into the sea?"

"Er... yes, but it was the demons—"

"Yeah, and I'm Pharaoh. Next please."

J: Fair enough, but you're forgetting the good stuff. What about Legion?

PJ: We'll get back to him in a minute if that's okay. First, I'd like to ask you about the guy who owned the pigs. How much do you think you cost him?

J: I'm a Messiah, not an accountant, so I couldn't give you a precise estimate.

PJ: That's okay, because we asked a number of butchers and hospitality experts to come up with a figure, and they said that an average pig can supply enough bacon for up to 500 bacon butties, so those 2000 pigs would give us a total of one million bacon butties. Now, if we conservatively price each bacon butty at, say, £1—

J: Oh no!

PJ: Oh yes. It means that thanks to your little swiney-in-the-briney stunt, that pig-farmer is out a cool million.

J: Not to mention bankruptcy and homelessness.

PJ: Probably.

J: Let's focus on Legion. His sanity returned and I sent him back home to tell everyone the joyous news of what God had done for him.

PJ: Despite him begging to stay with you. How come you do what the demons want but not what Legion wants? I suppose you said no to him because you couldn't say no to all that good publicity.

J: I prefer to call it 'spreading the good news'.

PJ: I notice you didn't send the pig-farmer back home to tell everyone the joyous news of what God had done for *him*.

J: Win some, lose some.

PJ: Except you missed a golden opportunity to win some, win some more.

J: How do you mean?

PJ: How come you didn't think to compensate that farmer?

J: Of course! It never even crossed my mind! After the pig disaster there just wasn't time to think straight, what with all those people urging me to get the hell out of their country.

PJ: I suppose we could put it down to yet more thoughtlessness... I mean, we've come *this* far.

J: There was so much I could have done, now I think of it.

PJ: You're 2000 years too late, one for every pig, but yes, you could have magicked a million out of thin air.

J: Or resurrected all those pigs from the sea.

PJ: You wouldn't even need to resurrect them if you'd made them walk on water instead.

J: Ha ha. What a sight that would have been!

PJ: But sadly, you didn't lift a finger to help.

J: Have you thought of an explanation yet for these poor decisions?

PJ: I'm working on it.

J: It'll need to be a whopper to cover all this.

PJ: Indeed. But let's move on to the disastrous environmental consequences.

J: You mean the pigless hillside?

PJ: No, I mean the pigful seaside. Have you any idea what that will do to the tourist industry?

J: What do you mean?

PJ: I mean, who's going to go snorkelling with 2000 bloated pig carcasses floating about? It's not like swimming with dolphins.

J: I see your point.

PJ: It's like a modern-day oil spill, but without the clean-up operation.

J: But won't the sea take care of this for us? It'll gradually break down the bodies and spread the tiny bits of pork throughout the lake.

PJ: Yes, and another thing in your favour is the fish. They'll eat all the little bits and clean it all up.

J: Oh my God!! Those pigs are unclean! This is a nightmare.

PJ: Don't worry yourself. After they've been in the water for a day or two, they'll be the cleanest pigs in the whole Middle East.

J: No, you don't understand. They're *ritually* unclean. Jews aren't allowed to eat pigs; they're not kosher.

PJ: But there's no rule against fish eating them, is there? I mean, fish aren't very religious, and you can't expect them to have read the Torah, hee hee.

J: You can laugh, but this is serious. There's a big fishing industry in Galilee — where do you think I got my disciples from? And when those fish are caught and sold in markets up and down Judaea, anyone who eats them will be eating bits of taboo pig. I'll have religiously contaminated the whole of the Holy Land!

PJ: Well, I can't take that seriously. We Gentiles see them as silly, arbitrary rules about menu choice. And I'm surprised at you. Aren't you the religious pioneer who wanted the Jews to ditch rules like these? What was it you said? Oh yes, "It's not what goes into the mouth that contaminates a man, but what comes out of it."

J: That's true, but it's one thing to preach against these rules, and quite another to sneak a ham sandwich into a Pharisee's lunch box when he's not looking.

PJ: Ah, I see what you mean.

J: It's so, so bad. But at least I have the comfort of knowing it can't get any worse.

PJ: Well, actually…

J: Please don't tell me there's more of this.

PJ: I'm afraid so.

J: But it's so unfair. It was only one small thoughtless decision that started all this. I gave those demons the gift of mercy, and this is how I'm repaid.

PJ: Well, it's the gift that keeps on giving, because you know what?

J: What?

PJ: Those demons are still out there. They didn't die with the pigs.

J: Of course! They're eternal evil spirits.

PJ: Yes, and they'll be looking for more bodies to possess.

J: And they liked the neighbourhood — first Legion, then the pigs — they'll be going back for more. They've got the taste for animals now.

PJ: That's right; after that wild roller-coaster ride into the sea they'll want to do it all over again and again with different animals. Can you picture what those demon jockeys will do with horses?

J: Farm after farm will go under.

PJ: The whole economy of the region will be in melt-down.

J: Surely things can't get any worse than that.

PJ: Well, actually…

J: You've got to be kidding. There's more?

PJ: One final thing.

J: Please put me out of my misery, Peremy.

PJ: It's Legion. When the demons have run out of animals, and you can walk across the Sea of Galilee on the corpses, they'll come looking for Legion.

J: And they'll find him because he'll still be there thanks to me! I refused his pleas to come with me and sent him back on a publicity drive.

PJ: Yes, and when they find him it'll be, "Home, Sweet Home." They'll never leave again.

J: That's it, Peremy. It's now or never. We've got to come up with a cover story right now or I'll never be able to show my face again, especially to Dad.

PJ: Is Joe still around?

J: The wood dude? No, not *him*. My *heavenly* Father. You know — God. Sometimes when I'm stressed, I call him Dad.

PJ: Jesus, you're a genius.

J: I am?

PJ: Yes, you've just given me the final bit of our cover story.

J: You mean you've thought of something!?

PJ: Yes, but you won't like it.

J: I don't care, as long as it works.

PJ: Okay, here goes. Your thoughtless decision to give the demons what they wanted was the result of…

J: Yes!?

PJ: Wait for it…

J: The result of what, for Christ's sake!?

PJ: Holiday madness!

J: Have you completely lost your mind!? It's not enough that we've got mad Legion and 2000 mad pigs on our hands. You want a mad Messiah as well? And who ever heard of a Messiah taking himself off on holiday? What are people going to think?

PJ: Look, it's not as if you're drinking margaritas by the pool; and 'holiday madness' is just an expression. It doesn't mean you're *really* insane.

J: What *does* it mean?

PJ: It means you're not quite yourself… a little off balance psychologically. Not enough to be *un*balanced, but just enough for you to make the odd thoughtless decision. It's the sort of irresponsible decision people are more likely to make on holiday.

J: I hear you. I'm still not sold on the holiday idea but go on.

PJ: Okay, here's the story. You're on holiday, checking out the Gadarene scene east of Galilee. It's your very first day, and you've just got off the ferry—

J: It was only a fishing boat.

PJ: Yes, but it ferried you across, so we'll call it the ferry. Trust me, it'll play better. Anyway, things have a different feel to them here; different scenery, different accent, different people — Gentiles. You're out of your comfort zone — like going from England to Wales… weird road signs, and all that. People tend to do silly things on holiday — things out of character, because they're not quite themselves.

J: You really think people will be understanding about my silly decision to help the demons just because it was made on holiday?

PJ: Well, it helps, but we need a bit more.

J: Like what?

PJ: You were drunk... and seasick.

J: Have you taken leave of your senses?

PJ: Okay, maybe that's too much. Let's tone it down a bit...You're the right side of drunk — tipsy — a little the worse for wear.

J: Let me stop you right there. This isn't going to work. There are too many unanswered questions.

PJ: Like what?

J: Like, 'Why am I drinking?' 'Why am I seasick when I've been sailing on that lake since I was a boy?' And, 'Why on earth do I need a holiday?'

PJ: Relax. When you hear the rest of the story all those questions will be answered.

J: Okay, but this better be good.

PJ: This'll work... now listen, here's the timeline: we're at the start of your career as Messiah. You've just been baptised by John the Baptist, and off you go into the wilderness, fasting for 40 days and 40 nights, and being tempted by Satan. After such a gruelling ordeal you emerge triumphant, but you're badly in need of some R and R to get your strength back. Now all you want is some time off for a bit of peace and quiet. However, no sooner are you back from your titanic struggle with Satan in the desert, when you discover you've got to go to this damned wedding party with your mum! Mums, eh? Anyway, you help out with the wine and you make this amazing high-octane hooch that any Hillbilly'd be proud of.

J: High-octane hooch?

PJ: Let's just say, as wine goes, it's super-unleaded. Anyway, it's your first drink...

J: But I'm thirty.

PJ: You're a late starter. Work with me here. You're drinking rocket fuel on 40 days of empty stomach. Like any teenager, you're still not sure of your limits, but you're wise enough to know when to stop — the right side of drunk — only two sheets to the wind instead of three. And the next morning you have a hangover.

J: Too much.

PJ: Okay, you're not *hung*over; you're *leant* over. Brain already on its third drum solo. And that's when you decide it would be a great idea to get into a boat and start that well-earned holiday. So, you set off... boat's bobbing, head's throbbing, throat's gobbing.

J: I get the picture.

PJ: By the time you get to the other side of the lake you're as green as a leprechaun who's just spent five hours in a cement mixer.

J: Whatever that is; but I'm not seasick!

PJ: The right side of seasick... enough to give you wobbly knees and a stomach that sounds like a dishwasher, but not enough to throw up.

J: Okay so far.

PJ: Well, you're no sooner off the ferryboat, tottering on your rubber legs and still reeling from the journey, when you're confronted by a stark-naked madman who's cornered the market in demons, and he's in your face, screeching at you at the top of his lungs. In that condition, and in those circumstances, it's amazing you didn't make an even bigger cock-up!

J: You really think people will understand?

PJ: Understand!? You'll be a hero! They'll just be glad you didn't press the nuclear button.

J: But won't people lose some respect for me?

PJ: Perhaps just a little, but it's well worth it, and believe it or not, it actually makes you seem a bit more human. Trust me; we've all been there, but at least most times we can cover it up.

J: But not me. I guess it was just bad luck it leaked out.

PJ: Bad luck, my ass! Normally what happens in Vegas, stays in Vegas. But that bastard, the Holy Ghost, ratted you out and blabbed about it all over the tabloids.

J: You mean, the gospels?

PJ: Yes, it's in three out of four.

J: Wow. So, the whole world knows about me and the demons. But at least I can now explain *why* I did them a favour.

PJ: Yes, I think we've got that covered. It only cost a few dents and scratches to your image. But we need to do something about the dire *consequences* of that decision.

J: But it's too late to change them now. You can't turn back the clock.

PJ: No, but it's not too late to distract people so they don't look too closely at them. We need a distraction that's as grim as those consequences, yet completely innocent in order to shift people's focus away from the horror of what you did.

J: What do you have in mind, Peremy?

PJ: You won't like it.

J: Would you stop with the 'You won't like it' routine and just tell me?

PJ: Dad jokes!

J: What are *they*?

PJ: They're excruciating jokes that dads make up for the pleasure of seeing their children squirm in mental torment. They're memorable for all the wrong reasons, but in your case, all the right reasons. We'll use them when we tell the story about Legion, because people will feel the pain of the dad jokes and remember *them* as opposed to the economic and environmental Armageddon you brought to the region.

J: Great! But I don't know any dad jokes.

PJ: No, but your dad does.

J: Who, Joe?

PJ: No! Not just any old dad will do. You need your heavenly Father. He's King of kings, Lord of lords, and Dad of dads, and if God himself can't give us the kind of gut-wrenching dad jokes we need, I don't know who can.

J: Okay, I'll ask him, but could you give me a couple of examples, so I know the sort of thing to ask for?

PJ: Right, I've got two... brace yourself... are you ready?

J: Ready.

PJ: They're doing a sequel to 'Gladiator'. It's going to be an epic about how the Romans invented central heating.

J: Oh? What's it called?

PJ: Radiator.

J: Ugh. That's awful. I see what you mean. What's the other one?

PJ: You know the website ancestry.com, where you can go to check out your family history?

J: Yes.

PJ: Well, Hillbillies have a website of their own for this.

J: They do?

PJ: Yes, it's called incestry.com

J: Ugh. That's terrible! I'm getting Golgotha flashbacks. Okay, you've convinced me. I'll ask my heavenly Dad, and we'll see what he comes up with. Can you give me a moment for a quick prayer?

PJ: Sure.

J: Oh, Father of mine

I killed 2000 swine.

Now I need to distract

From my pig-killing act.

So tell me a dad joke

To prove I'm no bad bloke.

PJ: You'll need more than one.

J: Send several to me

Please, A.S.A.P.

PJ: Why the poem?

J: If you say it with rhyme

Then you get it on time.

He likes it when people put in the extra effort.

PJ: Okay, Jesus, while we're waiting for the dad jokes to come through, there's something I've been meaning to ask you.

J: What's that?

PJ: Well, Legion was supposed to have thousands of demons, so there must be a way of counting them. But how on earth do you count demons?

J: That's easy. You go, one demon, two demons, three demons, four demons…

PJ: No, that's not what I mean. I mean, it's not like counting smarties. At least you can tell where one smartie ends and another begins, because they're physical and you can see them. But demons aren't physical and can't be seen.

J: Not with *normal* eyes; you must use the eyes of faith.

PJ: Really? And are those faith eyeballs set in the sockets of belief?

J: I'm sensing a bit of scepticism, Peremy.

PJ: Yes, I'm having trouble seeing with the eyes of faith because the brain of doubt is blocking my view.

J: How?

PJ: It's sitting right in front of me, wearing a big hat of disbelief.

J: You're just making stuff up.

PJ: Unlike you… and what about those Gentiles? They're unbelievers, yet they were calling him Legion before you even got there. How could they tell he had a lot of demons when they couldn't have been using the eyes of faith?

J: Er… perhaps it was a lucky guess.

PJ: Are you sure they weren't using the guess of faith?

J: And anyway, there's another way to tell how many demons you're dealing with. It's the different voices they use.

PJ: Yeah, but the problem with that is, how can you tell the difference between ten demons, and one demon who does impressions?

J: You use the ears of faith.

PJ: Don't tell me; if *they* don't work you can use the nose of faith. Please tell me there's a nose of faith!

J: Poke fun all you want, but the thing is, there's got to be a way to count demons, for if not, how do you know there's even one demon as opposed to none?

PJ: Jesus, that's exactly my point. If there's no way to count them, it doesn't make sense to say there's even one demon. It seems to me that trying to count demons is like trying to count rabies. If a dog has rabies it doesn't make sense to ask how many. Imagine the conversation:

"I'm afraid my dog has rabies."

"He must be raving mad then."

"Not at all. The other day I was examining him with the eyes of faith, and I only counted two rabies, but it's enough to give him a nervous tic. One raby makes him nervous—the other raby gives him the tic."

J: Are you saying my demon theory of mental illness is groundless?

PJ: Yes, like the heebie-jeebie theory of mental discomfort.

J: Are you telling me you can't count heebie-jeebies?

PJ: That's right.

J: What about the creeps?

PJ: Them too.

J: What about the willies?

PJ: Er… yes and no, but don't ask why.

J: But if there aren't any demons, what have I been casting out all this time? Don't you have demons these days?

PJ: No, we have science. We have brain tumours, epilepsy, post-traumatic stress disorder, dementia, and a thousand other things, but no demons.

J: Mmm… back in my day, we just had demons, demons, and more demons — and sin. They were simpler times.

PJ: Just one more question about demons.

J: What's that?

PJ: Why are demons always wanting to *possess* people? It's always demon *possession*, demon *possession*.

J: Because they're into home ownership. They prefer to own the homes they live in.

PJ: Ah, that's why you never hear of anyone suffering from demon rental.

J: Exactly... ooh, aah.

PJ: What's wrong, Jesus?

J: The dad jokes are starting to come through, but it's going to take another couple of minutes to get them all.

PJ: Okay, I'll try to keep you talking to take your mind off the pain.

J: Great! What would you like to talk about?

PJ: This. Can you read what Matthew says here in chapter 8 verse 28?

J: [Jesus reads Matt.8:28]: *"When he came to the other side, to the country of the Gadarenes, two demoniacs coming out of the tombs met him."* (Stops reading). TWO demoniacs! There were *two* of them!?

PJ: I thought we had problems counting demons, but it seems Matthew can't even count people. What a loser! He can't even count up to one without getting it wrong.

J: You're too hard on him. Maybe this was just a one-off.

PJ: Oh, that it was so, but no—he's got previous.

J: How do you mean?

PJ: Well, he was partly to blame for you having to double up on trees in your fig tree debacle.

J: *Incident*, fig tree *incident*.

PJ: And you remember when you healed that blind man near Jericho?

J: Yes, his name was Bartimaeus.

PJ: Well, Matthew has you healing two of them.

J: What's wrong with him? Is he cross-eyed or something?

PJ: There's more.

J: You're kidding.

PJ: No, it's no joke, but this next one's pretty funny.

J: What next one?

PJ: The one where he has you riding two donkeys at the same time.

J: What!? There must be some mistake!

PJ: Oh, that it was so, but no. It's during your triumphal entry into Jerusalem on Palm, (I mean Ass-riding), Sunday.

J: Show me where he says that.

PJ: It's right here in Matthew 21. Verse 7; [shows Jesus Matt.21:7]

J: [Jesus reads]: *"they brought the donkey and the colt, and put their cloaks on them, and he sat on them."* I can't believe it!

PJ: Try using the eyes of faith.

J: I'd have to do the splits to get my legs across two donkeys! That's quite a feat.

PJ: I'd have paid good money to see that. No wonder you drew a crowd.

J: But they came to see *me*, not a circus act.

PJ: Are you sure it wasn't your stunt double?

J: Eh?

PJ: Perhaps you stood on the donkeys, one foot on each. It's less exciting, but still worth seeing.

J: I told you, it was *me* they came to see, not someone doing donkey tricks.

PJ: Well, perhaps you're wrong to think it's always about *you*. Don't forget, there's no i in Mess... okay, bad example... You should remember there's no i in Saviou... For goodness sake! One more try... Remember there's no i in Chri... aw forget it!

J: Come on. Don't give up now.

PJ: Okay, I'll give it one last go… mmm… I've got it! Don't forget, there's no i in Jesus.

J: There is if you're French.

PJ: Ah, but what if you're English?

J: Then the i is in us.

PJ: That's it. I give up. You're smarter than the Holy Ghost.

J: That's not hard.

PJ: Hee hee. Okay, I think it's high time we got back to your double donkey trouble. Any ideas?

J: Maybe the solution is that I rode one donkey after the other in a sort of relay.

PJ: You mean like a Pony Express rider? That makes it exciting again.

J: Yes, but not fast like them. I'm not trying to outrun Crazy Horse, and it was only a mile or so.

PJ: It's getting boring again. If that's all you did, I'm surprised *anyone* turned up.

J: Forget the donkeys; what are we going to do about two Legions?

PJ: Mmm… What if Legion had an identical twin?

J: Who's also called Legion? No wonder he had mental problems.

PJ: You know, it's ironic. Matthew can't do basic maths, yet his name begins with Matth!

J: And he even manages to double up on 't's!

PJ: Good one Jesus.

J: Yeah, but we still haven't solved the two Legions problem. Mark and Luke say there's one, and Matthew says there are two. They *can't* all be right, yet they *must* all be right, because the Holy Ghost wrote them all and he'll never admit he's wrong—remember the murdered children?

PJ: How could I forget? Hey Jesus, I think I've got the answer!

J: What?

PJ: You're not going to like it.

J: Really? Do we have to do this again?

PJ: Fine; you know in the aftermath, after you heal Legion, the demons survive the mass pig-drowning and go on to destroy farm after farm?

J: Yes, thanks for reminding me.

PJ: Well, right at the end, the last thing they do is find Legion and possess him again. That's your cue...

J: (Light dawning) ... Of course! That's my cue to cast out the demons for a *second* time. Which means we can have our cake and eat it, because in one sense there's just one Legion, but in another sense, there are two, because I heal him *twice* at *different* times.

PJ: There *is* a price to pay for this solution though.

J: What price is that?

PJ: It means we'll have to double up on the pig massacre, the environmental catastrophe, and the economic wasteland. Oh, and there's one more thing.

J: You're beginning to sound like Columbo.

PJ: It also means you didn't learn a thing from your first mistaken decision and did exactly the same thing next time round.

J: Well then, let's hope those dad jokes work. I've got them all now.

PJ: Fantastic! Let's practise our lines. Here's what we do... I interview you again about Legion and all that, and you slip the dad jokes into your answers. If we keep it short and snappy, they'll never know what hit 'em.

J: Okay, Peremy. Fire away.

PJ: When you got off the boat you were met by a madman. Opinion differs about the number of demons he had. How many demons did you count?

J: 88.

PJ: The Gentiles called him Legion, but what did *you* call him?

J: Two fat ladies.

PJ: Figures… ha ha… Now, how would you describe your decision to help the demons?

J: I made a pig's ear of it.

PJ: Ughh. The jokes are beginning to work… So, what happened after the demons entered the pigs?

J: They ran down a steep embankment into the sea. You'll never guess what the locals call it.

PJ: What?

J: The Piggy Bankment.

PJ: Ughh. So, all those dead pigs must have caused a lot of pollution.

J: Yes, they say it's the biggest oink-spill in Galilean history.

PJ: Aaghhh… But what would you say to animal rights people who accuse you of murder?

J: I'd say it was hamicide, not homicide.

PJ: Urrrgghh… The pain's getting worse…Must keep going… Wine-producers are complaining they could have used all that wasted pig manure to fertilise their vines. What do you say to them?

J: It's just sow grapes.

PJ: Oooohhhrr. What about complaints that pigs are clogging the sea?

J: That's just a load of hogwash!

PJ: Oorrhhhgggzz… I can't take much more, Jesus.

J: Hang in there; just one more question to go.

PJ: Okay; after the pigs died, the demons were still out there. What do you think of the theory that they'll go on to invade farm after farm after farm?

J: It's just another Vietham Demono Theory.

PJ: Aaaarrrrrrgggghhh! Please, no more.

J: Relax. That's the lot.

PJ: Well, congratulations Jesus; that was so appalling it's bound to distract even the severest of critics from your pig massacre.

J: Thanks, Peremy; you've saved my bacon.

PJ: Aaaaarrrrrrgggggghhhhhhhhh!

Jesus Christ, ladies and gentlemen.

(Applause, as Jesus helps the now traumatised Peremy off the stage while the fade-out music plays, 'Oh I do like to be beside the seaside').

Luke. 24: 1 – 54 and Acts. 1: 1 – 11

Rocketman

('Space Oddity' by Bowie, is playing as Peremy comes on)

Peremy Jaxman (PJ). (To camera) — Tonight, ladies and gentlemen, we have a very special guest who claims to have actually travelled across the space-time continuum to another dimension. He has kindly taken time out from his very busy life spent sitting at the right hand of God and... er... that's it... just sitting... to come to the studio to answer some questions about his cosmic trip. That's right, you've guessed it; please give a big Earthling welcome to the man himself, Jesuuus Chrrrist!

(Loud applause as Jesus comes on stage, shakes Peremy's hand, and sits down; walk-on music is the theme from 'Doctor Who'.)

PJ: Jesus, I'd like to start by asking you about your alleged Ascension from Planet Earth to heaven.

Jesus (J): What do you mean 'alleged'?

PJ: Sorry, I thought that since Luke's is the only gospel to mention it, that perhaps he'd got it wrong.

J: No way!

PJ: Okay, but it can't have been all that important since the other three didn't see fit to give it any airtime.

J: Of course it was important, otherwise I'd still be stranded down here. There was no point hanging around (ha ha) once I'd done my bit.

PJ: And I must say our studio audience, along with the viewers at home, really appreciate the effort you put in. What a trooper, ladies and gentlemen!

(Applause)

J: (Looking sheepish and a little embarrassed). Oh now, it was nothing really. Any half-decent god would have done the same.

PJ: Well, jolly well done anyway. Now, getting back to your Ascension, could you tell us *when* you did it?

J: Yeah, it was 40 days after Zoom Tomb Sunday. I rise from the dead and chill out with the disciples till it's time to return to base. Luke writes about it in Acts chapter 1.

PJ: You mean he wrote his gospel *and* Acts!?

J: (Doing a cowboy accent). Yep, good ol' 'Two-Book Luke' — fastest pen in the West.

PJ: (Joining in). Reckon so... So, how'd ya know it was time to saddle up and ride off into the sunset? (Switching back). Did you sense that the, er... how shall I put it... that the, er... Mother Ship was calling you home, you know, like in 'Independence Day'?

J: You've been watching too many movies, Peremy. I'm not Jeff Goldblum.

PJ: Fair enough, but if it wasn't like that, just what *was* it like? I'm sure we'd all be fascinated to hear exactly *how* you did it.

J: How do you mean?

PJ: Well, for example, did God suck you up, like a vacuum cleaner?

J: No, it was more of a hover than a hoover.

PJ: I see. Well, perhaps God used attraction instead. Were magnets involved?

J: Do I look like a metal Messiah to you?

PJ: Er... no, but they say your persona exudes a certain magnetism. Couldn't God have used a *spiritual* magnet to pull you up by your personality?

J: Well, as *attractive* as that sounds, that's not how it worked.

PJ: What about rocket power? Did you have a count-down before you blasted off?

J: No, I'd look ridiculous; Messiahs don't 'blast off' as you call it... it was more like silently gliding up into the air under my own steam.

PJ: Wow! The Ascension was steam-driven!? That'll attract the fans.

J: It wasn't meant to be an air display, and anyway the steam was metaphorical.

PJ: But metaphorical steam drives nothing. Do you see where I'm going with this?

J: Not to heaven, at this rate, ha ha!

PJ: Good one, Jesus. Now, you used the phrase, 'silently gliding'. That reminds me of how a train pulls out of a station. Was it a bit like that?

J: Yes, but not a steam train — and it was vertical not horizontal. That's an important point.

PJ: Of course, otherwise it would be called 'The Orbit' instead of 'The Ascension'.

J: Yes. And an orbiting Messiah would look stupid. I'd be like a low-flying aircraft. People would wave at me every time I came round...

PJ: Yeah, that would be pretty funny.

J: Not to mention embarrassing. I mean, what's the point of going round in circles like some sort of holy satellite? And when would I eat?

PJ: Well, I suppose if you slowed down you could sign autographs and pick up a burger.

J: What kind of a life is that, spent eating burgers and signing autographs?

PJ: Maybe you should ask Elvis. And isn't it better than just sitting?

J: But look *where* I sit... Anyway, we in the trinity had discussed how to avoid a vaudeville Ascension and we thought a bit of hovering followed by a slow upwards glide would do the trick.

PJ: Now, since you knew you'd be travelling upwards, did you take any precautions against embarrassing revelations?

J: What do you mean?

PJ: Well, as you're making your way upwards, wouldn't the people on the ground be able to see up your robe? That sort of thing tends to detract from the solemnity of the occasion.

J: It wasn't a big deal. They were all men on the ground anyway, and once you've been to the gents a few times you stop being self-conscious about your bits.

PJ: Genital Jesus, meek and mild... it has a ring to it.

J: Can we move on to something a bit more edifying?

PJ: Of course... What did it feel like to be the first man in space?

J: Actually, I wasn't the first. If you remember, a few hundred years earlier Elijah was taken up into heaven in a chariot of fire.

PJ: I see, but if it was made of fire, wouldn't he have just fallen through the bottom?

J: No, it was solid fire.

PJ: Solid fire, eh? Good one. So, it was sort of like a cartoon cloud you can walk on?

J: Yes, except this was real. God doesn't do cartoon chariots.

PJ: So, if it was real fire, did God provide him with an asbestos suit so he didn't arrive in heaven ready-roasted?

J: No, it was the sort of fire that doesn't burn.

PJ: Fire that doesn't burn, eh? Another good one. So, it was sort of like a cartoon fire.

J: Yes, except this was real.

PJ: Amazing! I've never seen a real fire that's solid and doesn't burn. Isn't that what we call fiction?

J: I call it a miracle.

PJ: I call it metaphorical.

J: Can we get back to my Ascension?

PJ: You're right. I apologise; we shouldn't get distracted by an ascension which, not only was the *first* of its kind, but which was showier, and more spectacular than yours.

[Jesus sits there quietly bristling]

PJ: (Trying to appease Jesus). But at least not needing a chariot must be some compensation for coming in second.

J: You're missing the point. It wasn't a race. I just had to get back to heaven, that's all.

PJ: Of course. Now tell me, how did you manage to survive the trip through outer space without a space suit or oxygen tank? Did you wear a thermal vest and hold your breath?

J: No. I went so fast I was there in no time.

PJ: Wow! I bet the G-force must have been enormous, you know, when you accelerated out of Earth's atmosphere… so, once you got to heaven you could breathe again?

J: Yes.

PJ: There's air in heaven then? Is it air-conditioned? Does it have an atmosphere like Earth?

J: Hard to say. Up until Elijah and I went there physically heaven only contained spirits — angels, souls, God — you know the sort of thing; well, as you know, they don't need to breathe.

PJ: So, since you both have bodies, do you think God has the air pumped in just for you two?

J: That would make sense. And it would also keep Elijah's chariot alight.

PJ: Why would cartoon fire need air? Tell me, does he ever let you have a go on it?

J: I think you're getting distracted again.

PJ: You're right. So, what was it like when you finally touched down in heaven? Did you use a parachute to break your fall?

J: No. If I'd secretly stuffed a parachute under my robe it would have given me a hunch.

PJ: Ha ha, like a holy Quasimodo… Actually, come to think of it, you wouldn't need one…

J: Well, no one *needs* a hunch.

PJ: No, I mean you wouldn't need a *parachute,* because there's no gravity in heaven.

J: That's right — only levity. It's a very light-hearted place.

PJ: Quite. Now Jesus, before we finish the interview, I need to ask you about something that's been troubling me all the way through.

J: What's that, Peremy?

PJ: It's 'Two-Book Luke'. I think he's been spending too much time with, er… 'One-Book Matthew'.

J: Why do you think that?

PJ: Well, you know your Ascension?

J: I believe I *have* heard of it, yes.

PJ: Luke has you down for *two* of them.

J: What!? That can't be!

PJ: I'm afraid it does be. All the clues point that way.

J: What clues? And when was this other Ascension supposed to have happened?

PJ: On Zoom Tomb Sunday.

J: Zoom Tomb Sunday? That's 40 days too soon!

PJ: Maybe we should re-name it "Zoom Too Soon Tomb Sunday".

J: (Sarcastically). That's hilarious. Look, forget the label — what about these clues you were talking about? Are you sure they lead to an Ascension on the very day I'm resurrected?

PJ: I'm afraid so. Here's the timeline, and it's all in Luke chapter 24. First, you rise from the dead…

J: Yeah, I remember I got up early that morning.

PJ: Later the same day, probably early afternoon, you join two of your followers on a seven-mile hike from Jerusalem to Emmaus.

J: Yeah, we were chatting away, and the funny thing was, they didn't recognise me till we got there. I remember, we'd just started eating dinner when they clocked me.

PJ: That's when you go into your Invisible Man act, and suddenly disappear. This would be around dusk, say, 6.00 p.m.

J: That sounds right... er... Still no Ascension?

PJ: No, you're okay so far. Now, the next thing that happens is that these two scramble back to Jerusalem as fast as their legs will carry them, to tell the other disciples what's happened. How long do you think it would take them?

J: Let's see, it's seven miles, and they're scrambling. Oh, I'd say about a couple of hours at most.

PJ: That sounds reasonable. So, it's around 8.00 p.m. when they arrive and start into their story. And it's while this is going on that you suddenly appear in their midst, like a rabbit out of a hat.

J: Yeah, that was funny. I said, "Peace be with you", and they nearly wet themselves. They thought it was a ghost! It reminded me of that stunt... er, miracle I pulled on the Sea of Galilee when I walked on the water.

PJ: Ha ha, yeah that was a scream... But we're getting distracted again...Anyway, after your disciples have presumably changed their underwear, and resumed a suitably serious yet joyful demeanour, you have another good chat together.

J: Yeah, that would have taken up another couple of hours I suppose. Still no Ascension?

PJ: No, but you've run out of luck, because it's just about to happen. It must be about 10.00 p.m. now when you all leave for Bethany, about two miles away. The journey there would take us to around 11.00 p.m. — time for Ascension number one. Here, read it for yourself. It's in Luke. 24: verses 51 and 52. (Hands Jesus a Bible).

J: (Reading). *"Then he led them out as far as Bethany, and lifting up his hands, he blessed them. While he was blessing them, he withdrew from them and was carried up into heaven."* Oh my God! Two Ascensions! And this one at night. It looks so, so bad.

PJ: On the contrary, I'd have thought a night-time launch would look pretty cool.

J: What am I going to do? This is a total disaster.

PJ: Yeah; another load of bollocks cooked up by the Holy Ghost — and what makes it worse is that you can't wriggle out of it by using your 'doubling-up-on-stuff' ploy like you did with the fig tree debacle...

J: *Incident*, fig tree *incident*...

PJ: Because you're *already* double-booked on Ascensions.

J: And we can't say one of the two accounts is wrong because the Holy Ghost wrote both, and he'll never admit he's wrong. Remember the murd—

PJ: I'm way ahead of you.

J: What's he playing at?

PJ: You mean, the Holy Ghost? Yeah, no wonder that blockhead's bottom of the class at number 3. But you've got to hand it to him — I mean, *two* Ascensions! He didn't even break sweat.

J: He's made me look ridiculous. I mean, to make the whole thing work, I'd have to ascend to heaven the first time, and then return *immediately* to planet Earth so I can spend the 40 days with my disciples before taking off again on my next

Ascension. But the problem is, why on earth did I go in the first place?

PJ: Hmm… How about: 'You were still on a high from the Resurrection'? You started rising from the dead, and simply kept on rising… you know, like a helium balloon.

J: No, that won't work. It doesn't cover the hike to Emmaus.

PJ: Hmm… Let alone the other stunts you pulled that day. We need to have another think.

J: If only there were another way to explain it. (Thinks)… hmm… er… um…

PJ: What about… er…? No, that won't work; I'd get lynched… How about… um…? No, that won't work either — only Holocaust deniers, or the Holy Ghost, would be stupid enough to buy it… hmmm… (light dawning) … Ah hah! I've got it! Hey Jesus, I think you're in luck.

J: You mean you've thought of something!?

PJ: Yes, but you won't like it.

J: Here we go again. *Of course* I won't like it. You know it. I know it. By now, everybody knows it — but you're going to tell me anyway, right? So, what's the 'it' I won't like?

PJ: Okay, here 'it' comes… your first Ascension was a genuine ascension attempt, but it didn't quite work out.

J: Why not?

PJ: Because when you got there, you couldn't get into heaven.

J: Why, what's the problem?

PJ: Er… you couldn't get through the door.

J: Why on earth not?

PJ: You forgot your keys.

J: (Jesus explodes). What the hell kind of a cover story is that!?

PJ: I told you you wouldn't like it.

J: You need your head examined. And who'd be crazy enough to trust a Messiah to take them to heaven, when he can't even get in himself!? It's insane. Oh, and tell me this — just *where* did I leave my keys?

PJ: You gave them to Peter before you went.

J: What makes you think that?

PJ: Because it says so here. Read what you say to Peter in Matthew 16: verse 19.

J: (Jesus reads). *"I will give you the keys of the kingdom of heaven; and whatever you bind on earth will be bound in heaven, and whatever you loose on earth will be loosed in heaven."*

PJ: So, what do you think?

J: It's a nice try, but I don't think people will buy it.

PJ: Why not?

J: Too many problems.

PJ: Such as?

J: The meaning's not clear for a start. What on earth's all this binding and loosing business? And how do we know that "the keys of the *kingdom* of heaven" are the same as "the keys of heaven" that I supposedly need to get into the damned place? And it also says that I *will* give him the keys, but it doesn't say *when* this will happen. Suppose it happens too late, say, *after* my first Ascension instead of *before* it.

PJ: Jesus, you're worrying over nothing. Trust me, this'll work. Look, if everyone's arguing over the meaning because it's not at all clear, that means our interpretation that they're the exact same keys, is as good as anyone else's. Relax... you gave him your keys and that's that. Who can prove us wrong? And don't worry about *when* you gave them to him. That's not a problem because it *can't* have been too late. You see, you *had* to have given them to him *before* your first Ascension, because that's precisely what caused the problem in the first place. If it had been *after* it, (i.e. 'too late', so that he wouldn't have had them on him when you went back to Earth to get them from him), you'd have been able to get into heaven anyway, and have no need to go back for them because the keys would still have been in your possession!

J: But what about all that binding and loosing baloney?

PJ: That's the beauty of our cover story. It doesn't matter a damn what it means because whatever it is, Peter won't be able to do it once you take your keys off him. Just make sure he doesn't get his hands on them during the 40 days you're on Earth between Ascensions.

J: You know, it just might work!

PJ: Of course it will work, and there's the added bonus that it makes you look even more like one of us—I mean, who hasn't forgotten their keys at some time or other?

J: That's right! It's a human foible, not a sin. I'm sure folks will understand.

PJ: Yes, and they'll love you all the more for it.

J: That's fantastic!

PJ: There's only one problem, Jesus.

J: What's that?

PJ: The Second Coming has already happened. It was when you came back for your keys.

J: (Dumbfounded). But that means billions of Christians have been waiting in vain for thousands of years, for a bus that's already been and gone!

PJ: Well, Jesus, I'm afraid that's all we have time for...

J: But... but... er...

PJ: Thank you so much for coming into the studio to talk to us. It's been a blast, and you've been a wonderful guest. (Turning to the audience) — Ladies and gentlemen, will you please show your appreciation for Jesus Christ, the Son of God!

(Uproarious applause, as Jesus, in a state of catatonic shock, is helped off stage by Peremy).

(Fade out with, 'Fly me to the Moon' by Sinatra.)

Acts. 4: 32 – 5: 11

Moneytheism

PJ: Good evening ladies and gentlemen. Welcome to the show. Tonight, I'll be talking to a very special guest; probably *the* most famous disciple of them all. Please give it up for the rock on which the church was built, yes, it's none other than Saint Peter himself!

(Applause as Peter comes on stage. Walk-on music is 'Money, Money, Money' by Abba)

PJ: Welcome to the show Pete.

P: Thanks. It's good to be here Peremy.

PJ: Now, you were the very first CEO of God's business venture, weren't you?

P: I was the very first head of God's church, if that's what you mean.

PJ: Yes, that's exactly what I mean.

P: I wouldn't really call it a business. Despite its enormous wealth you won't find the church on the FTSE 100.

PJ: I understand. Better to stay under the radar as a "charity" (air quotes).

P: I wouldn't really call it a charity.

PJ: And yet every single day millions of people across the world simply hand over their money to the church. No invoices, no taxes, no advertising, and you don't have to earn any of it. How on earth did you wangle that?

P: What can I say? Jesus himself gave me the job, so he must have seen me as a safe pair of hands.

PJ: Don't sell yourself short, Pete. You're much more than that. You're a financial genius!

P: How do you mean?

PJ: The effortless way you separate people from their money. Millions washing into the church's coffers every day; trillions invested in art and real estate. That makes it one of the richest organisations on Earth. I think that's all down to you. You were there at the start.

P: No, it's all down to Jesus. *He* should get the credit, because the church follows *his* example, not mine.

PJ: Boy, then Jesus must have been absolutely *rolling* in it. Just how much was he worth?

P: Er... nothing. He didn't have a penny.

PJ: Not a cash man, eh? It must have all been tied up in property and art investments.

P: Uh... not exactly. To tell you the truth, he had nothing but the clothes he stood up in.

PJ: But the money must be *somewhere*... Ah, his *clothes*! That's it, isn't it? I'm guessing, Gucci sandals and Armani robe, huh? I bet he owned a fashion house!

P: (emphatically). Peremy, Jesus had no money at all!

PJ: You mean he was skint?

P: Stoney broke.

PJ: Wow! Then I was right; the church must be following *your* example, not his.

P: *My* example!? What did *I* do?

PJ: Don't tell me you've forgotten all about your New Testament 'get rich quick' scheme.

P: What are you talking about? What 'get rich quick' scheme?

PJ: Now don't be coy. Don't you remember that married couple, Ananias and Sapphira? You were — how shall I put it — embroiled in a financial dispute with them. It was about 2000 years ago, not long after Jesus handed the business over to you and returned to headquarters.

P: I have a vague recollection of the incident. But what's that got to do with the church's *current* wealth?

PJ: It's got everything to do with it. It was during that financial dispute that you had them killed on the spot for not putting enough money in the collection plate... *pour encourager les autres n'est pas*, eh Pierre? I bet when news of *that* got out, church donations went through the roof!

P: You must understand, I didn't do it for the money.

PJ: Perish the thought. But more money came in as a result, right?

P: Er... yes, I suppose so. The whole church was terrified.

PJ: I'm sure it was. If you want people to empty their pockets there's nothing like a bit of terror to get the job done.

P: 'Terror' is such an ugly word. I prefer to call it fear, as in 'the fear of the Lord'.

PJ: Quite right. I'm sure if we start calling them fearists instead of terrorists it will make all the difference in the fight to make our streets safe... now, let's get back to Ananias and Sapphira. Did you manage to get hold of the bit of money they kept back from you?

P: Well, they were no longer around to stop us, so... what do *you* think?

PJ: I think it was a stunning piece of financial wizardry!

P: Thank you.

PJ: So, you managed to get every last penny out of the murdered couple.

P: It was a judicial execution, not a murder.

PJ: Of course. And many would sympathise with your point of view — ISIS, the IRA, Nero.

P: Whatever, but money wasn't the motive for the killings.

PJ: So you keep saying. Can I ask what you did with the bodies?

P: Some of our young men carried them out and buried them.

PJ: Now that's what I call 'cash-and-carry'.

P: Look, I told you, it wasn't about the money.

PJ: Then why did you do it?

P: They lied to me.

PJ: That bad, eh? You old softy! Death's too good for them. But tell me, what did they lie to you about?

P: They lied about the money. They'd sold some property, but instead of giving *all* the money to the church, they secretly kept some back for themselves, yet they told me they hadn't.

PJ: This clearly merits instant death. But didn't the jury consider a fine instead? It would have brought in more *money*. (said greedily).

P: I'm afraid not.

PJ: I see. So, it was a unanimous vote for the death penalty.

P: Actually, there *was* no jury.

PJ: But this husband and wife are on trial for their lives. What did their defence counsel have to say in mitigation?

P: Mmm… they weren't allowed any defence counsel.

PJ: You mean they had no legal representation at all?

P: None to speak of.

PJ: So… then… none.

P: Er, yeah… none.

PJ: Who was the prosecuting counsel?

P: Uh… that would be me.

PJ: And the judge?

P: Er… also me.

PJ: So you were judge, jury, prosecutor *and* executioner. You're a one-man Old Bailey… Can you tell me how many witnesses were called to give evidence?

P: Let me see… er, none.

PJ: That's convenient. No need for any of that messy cross-examination stuff.

P: Yes, it's a real time-saver.

PJ: No doubt. But where's the justice if you don't use any witness evidence to back it up?

P: You don't need witness evidence if you *already* know what the verdict will be.

PJ: Wow! You had *prior* knowledge of the result? But if you were so certain of the outcome, you must have had cast-iron proof from another source.

P: That's right.

PJ: Let me guess… now, what would substantiate the charge of lying? Ah, I've got it. You managed to get hold of the receipts from the sale of the property, along with their bank statements, and compared those with the money they gave you.

P: Nice try, but no. There wasn't anything like that. Guess again.

PJ: I know… you got confessions out of them. They came clean and told all.

P: Wrong again.

PJ: Well Pete, I'm all out of ideas. I mean, what other evidence could there possibly be that's so strong it makes it an open-and-shut case?

P: I didn't need any evidence, because God had already secretly told me what they'd done!

PJ: What!? That's your cast-iron proof!?

P: Absolutely! God never lies.

PJ: Fascinating! So it was *God* who grassed them up. I never figured Jesus for a snitch.

P: God saw to it that justice was done.

PJ: Is that so? But how could you tell it was really God's voice in your head and not your own imagination?

P: There are ways.

PJ: But we can't test any of these ways to see if they're reliable, can we?

P: Correct. You just have to trust me.

PJ: I thought as much. Evidence isn't your thing, is it? You know, Thomas Hobbes once said, "When a man claims God spoke to him in a dream, all he means is that he dreamt God spoke to him."

P: And how does Hobbes know that?

PJ: Ah… you'll just have to trust him.

P: That's a cheap shot.

PJ: It's not nice being on the receiving end, is it? We need *publicly available* evidence to stop cranks who claim to hear

God's voice being taken seriously as witnesses in courts of law.

P: A court of God's law is different to a court of man's law.

PJ: You can say that again. In God's court you're guilty till proven guilty. No evidence, no jury, no legal representation, no appeals, no witnesses. In short, no rights. Just an ecclesiastical judge pronouncing a death sentence based solely on what the voices in his head are telling him.

P: You think it looks bad, huh?

PJ: Have you heard of something called 'The Inquisition'?

P: Er… no.

PJ.: Well, I think you may have started it.

P: Perhaps… after all, I *was* quite inquisitive. I asked Ananias more than once why he'd lied.

PJ: And what did he say in his defence?

P: Nothing.

PJ: Ah, the silent type, was he?

P: Yes… he dropped dead before he could reply — and the dead are definitely the silent type.

PJ: You mean to say that sentence was carried out *before* he could defend himself? *Before* the trial was even over?? In fact, come to think of it, the trial had barely begun!

P: I know it *looks* bad…

PJ: How long did the trial actually last?

P: About 15 seconds…Okay, it looks *really* bad…

PJ: You think!! Hey… it's just occurred to me — how could he possibly lie if he never actually got a chance to speak?

P: Well, it was a sort of *acted* lie.

PJ: You don't say.

P: Yes. You see, for some time prior to this, it was the norm for all church members to sell all their property and assets and give all the money to the apostles.

PJ: You mean the church authorities — people like yourself.

P: Yes, and then we would distribute the money held in our central funds according to people's needs. So, everyone ended up owning nothing at all, no private property of their own, and the money was shared with everyone.

PJ: Sounds like a Marxist's wet dream.

P: What?

PJ: Oh, nothing.

P: My point is that selling all you had and giving all your money to us — no holding back — was expected of everyone. It was the done thing, and it was official church economic policy, so to speak. And since it was the behaviour we expected of people, we assumed that Ananias, and his wife Sapphira, would do the same as everyone else, and when they didn't, our expectations weren't fulfilled, so we interpreted their behaviour as the equivalent of lying.

PJ: It sounds like they were merely nonconformists, executed in a 'show trial' for not toeing the Party line. That's enough to impress even Stalin.

P: Who?

PJ: Listen comrade, did it ever occur to you that perhaps they simply disagreed with your economic policy?

P: No. Why would anyone disagree? What could possibly be wrong with it?

PJ: Well, for starters, if you're doing this to help the poor by spreading the money around, you make the problem worse by adding to the poor those who have sold everything and given it all to you. They are now part of the problem, and you end up giving them back most of the money they gave you in the first place, because your economic policy made them voluntarily homeless and destitute. And what happens when your capital fund runs out because none of your former donors can continue to donate due to destitution, but are instead constantly drawing money out for their own needs; needs they would have been able to meet themselves if they hadn't already sold off all their money-making assets. People who were formerly self-sufficient by renting their property out, or farming their fields, or running their own shops, will forever be in thrall to the church because they sold their means of making a living in return for the privilege of begging favours from you.

P: Yes, I see the problem. The money keeps getting smaller and smaller, while the needs keep getting bigger and bigger. I think the solution is firstly, to invest our capital before it gets too low so we can get a return on our investment, and secondly, to keep on expanding by attracting more customers... er, donors... I mean converts. That way, we keep the money rolling in.

PJ: And you say you're not a business. Perhaps all that Ananias and Sapphira were guilty of was simply wondering why people can't be trusted to make their own decisions concerning their money and goods instead of being compelled, on pain of death, to hand over all their wealth and power to the church.

P: But you're just trying to second-guess their thoughts. You don't know this.

PJ: Yes, and now we'll never know because you had them killed before they could explain. By the way, how much money did *you* put in? There's no record of any donations from *you*.

P: Er… nothing.

PJ: You give nothing, yet you're happy to rake it all in and kill anyone who dares to keep a few quid back for themselves. I bet you're a big Al Capone fan.

P: I'm sensing a bit of negativity there, Peremy. You make it sound like a protection racket. And who's Big Al Capone?

PJ: It's just Al… mmm… the English lesson will have to wait. Now, did you manage to find out why they kept some of the money back?

P: Yes, it was for themselves.

PJ: I know, but could it have been to buy medicine for a sick relative, or to pay for their children's education? Did they have any children?

P: I don't know.

PJ: So, for all you know, you may have made a few orphans along with your two corpses.

P: But they lied.

PJ: Shocking! … hey, wait a minute. Aren't you the guy who lied about not knowing Jesus? I see *you're* still alive. How come God didn't rub *you* out?

P: That was different.

PJ: Too right it was different. You deny the Son of God not once, but *three times* to save your own skin, yet you remain alive so you can kill others whose only crime is to withhold a few coins from the church. That *is* different. At least Pontius Pilate had the decency to wash his hands.

P: I'm sensing more negative vibes. Aren't you happy with God's justice?

PJ: There's no fooling you, eh Pete?

P: You're not happy with me either, are you?

PJ: You got me again!

P: Listen, I'm just God's messenger — his servant. Don't shoot the messenger.

PJ: Are you claiming innocence?

P: Let's just remind ourselves that I didn't actually kill Ananias and Sapphira; God did it with a miracle, right on cue.

PJ: But you were the one who gave him his cue. You were his front man and condoned the whole thing. You might not have done the deed, but you were Master of Ceremonies and cheerleader rolled into one.

P: Well, if you think about it, it was really *God's* gig. It was *his* power that killed them, and *his* rule they broke.

PJ: It was a seedy little scene, and you're trying to weasel out of it. You've got form... remember?

P: Hear me out. You've missed something important.

PJ: Like what? God killed them because they broke his rule about lying. That's your story isn't it? What's missing?

P: What's missing is that it's not just a rule about lying per se. It's a very special rule to do with lying *to the Holy Ghost*.

PJ: So? What's the big deal about that?

P: It's the only sin that will never be forgiven.

PJ: You're kidding! Never ever?

P: Never ever.

PJ: I thought *all* sins could be forgiven.

P: Not this one.

PJ: How do you know? Has God been whispering in your ear again?

P: No. Jesus said so. It's in the Bible. Look up Matthew 12: vs 31 to 32.

PJ: Let me check (Finds the reference and starts to read):

"And so, I tell you that people can be forgiven any sin and any evil thing they say, but whoever says evil things against the Holy Spirit will not be forgiven. Anyone who says something against the Son of Man can be forgiven; but whoever says something against the Holy Spirit will not be forgiven — now or ever."

P: Now do you believe me?

PJ: Er... yes, but it doesn't make any sense. How come you can get away with saying evil things against Jesus, who's God's number two, but you're screwed if you target number three? Surely it should be the other way round.

P: It's a mystery.

PJ: Who put these words in Jesus's mouth anyway?

P: It was the Holy Ghost himself; he helped Matthew write them.

PJ: Why am I not surprised? Mystery solved.

P: How do you mean?

PJ: Let's put it like this: if there was no penalty for insulting the queen, but you got the death penalty for insulting Prince Charles that would be mystifying — why can you insult number one but not number two? It doesn't make any sense until you discover that it was none other than Prince Charles who made this rule up. Don't you see? The Holy Ghost is probably pissed at always being third in line — always the bronze medal, never silver or gold — so he makes this shit up and slips it into the Bible to get one over on the other two.

P: You're being very cynical.

PJ: Am I? Let's see. Apparently, I can be forgiven if I fuck a kid, or tell Jesus to stick his cross up his arse, but if I dare to suggest that the Holy Ghost is a bit of a wanker, then I'm without hope — forever doomed to burn in hell fire. Does that sound reasonable to you?

P: You're looking for 'reasonable' in religion? Were you born yesterday?

PJ: You're right. What was I thinking?

P: And be careful what you say about the Holy Ghost. He's very thin-skinned.

PJ: I'm not afraid of that tosser! What about free speech?

P: He doesn't believe in it. And I've got a voice in my ear telling me your soul is lost forever.

PJ: Pete, wake up and smell the bullshit. These are holy, ghost stories they use to scare little children… Now, there's one more thing I'd like to ask you about.

P: What's on your mind, Peremy?

PJ: You agree that the unforgivable sin is saying evil things against the Holy Ghost — trashing his character, insulting him — stuff like that, right?

P: Right.

PJ: Well, the thing is, neither Ananias nor Sapphira actually said any nasty stuff *against* the Holy Ghost. They never criticised him or slagged him off in any way. In fact, they never so much as mentioned him. Ananias didn't breathe a word, and his wife merely told *you* a lie about the money. What on earth has it got to do with the Holy Ghost?

P: Yes, but what you don't understand is that when anyone lies to me, they lie to God…

PJ: Humility's not your strong suit, is it?

P: As I was saying, lying to me is the same as lying to God, therefore they both lied to the Holy Ghost, which means they committed the unpardonable sin.

PJ: Hang on a minute. That doesn't follow. If you lie to God there's only a one in three chance, you're lying to the Holy Ghost bit. How do you know they weren't lying to the Father or the Son instead? Which would mean they're home free.

P: I know because God told me.

PJ: And I bet I know which bit did the telling; the Holy Ghost... right? The pair of you are as thick as thieves. You should both sign up for some counselling.

P: But why?

PJ: You're hearing voices, and as for him, he's got a chip on one shoulder and an inferiority complex on the other.

P: Prayer is the answer, not counselling.

PJ: Prayer... you mean, talking back to the voices?

P: You wouldn't understand.

PJ: You're right, I'm not a psychotherapist.

P: Look, it makes sense to think it was the Holy Ghost speaking to me because he's the part of God whom Jesus sent to comfort the church after he was gone.

PJ: And he's done a wonderful job. Having all that money must be a great comfort.

P: Whatever; the thing is, in lying to me Ananias and Sapphira lied to the Holy Ghost, and thus committed the unforgivable sin. That's why they had to die.

PJ: No, they didn't. According to that passage I read out, Jesus never said that lying *to* the Holy Ghost was the unforgivable sin. According to him, the unforgivable sin is saying *evil things **against*** the Holy Ghost. These aren't the same thing. Lying *to* someone isn't the same as lying *about* them.

P: What, not even a teeny bit?

PJ: Not even a teeny-*weeny* bit. The first is a mere lie; the second is slander.

P: But slanders are lies, so that makes them the same thing, doesn't it?

PJ: No. All slanders are lies, but not all lies are slanders.

P: What are you talking about?

PJ: Look, it's the same as saying all horses are animals but not all animals are horses. They're not the same thing, because if they were, that would mean that since a horse is an animal, and a pig is an animal, a pig must be a horse.

P: Ahh! I think I see your point. Since pigs are definitely animals, yet they're obviously not horses, being a horse can't be the same thing as being an animal.

PJ: Exactly. And the very same logic applies to lying and slander. Look at it this way; if I tell the Holy Ghost that Sitting Bull was Irish, then I merely lie *to* him. It's just a lie without being a slander. But if I spread the lie that the Holy Ghost gets his kicks from blow-torching cats, then I *am* guilty of slander by saying evil things *against* him. My point is, telling the lie that you gave all your money to the church, when in fact you didn't, does not amount to saying evil things against the Holy Ghost...

P: In the same way that saying, "There's a horse" does not amount to saying, "There's a pig".

PJ: Precisely! It doesn't even come close. They're talking about their personal finances in relation to the church authorities without even thinking about the Holy Ghost, in the same way that you can talk about horses without even thinking about pigs.

P: (realisation dawning) … But, if what you say is true, that would mean they *didn't* commit the unforgivable sin, and therefore didn't deserve to die.

PJ: It would appear so, and it would also appear that the Holy Ghost doesn't understand what he wrote.

P: Oh no…! Ananias and Sapphira! I'll have to haul them both out of hell.

PJ: Well, look on the bright side — they've only been sizzling for 2000 years.

P: Oh my God! What'll Jesus say when I tell him?

PJ: Why not deny it? You're good at that.

P: No. Jesus will find out sooner or later. I'd better come clean.

PJ: That'll make a nice change. And on that note, ladies and gentlemen, let's give Saint Peter a big round of applause for being such a good sport, and wish him the best of luck when he spills his guts to the Lord.

(Applause as Peter, looking stunned, stumbles off stage while the Beatles round things off with 'Can't buy me Love').

How to Write a Cracking good Miracle Story

Scene: *Nazareth Conference Centre*

Time: *Around AD90*

(Applause, as the compere comes onto the stage and addresses the audience. (Walk-on music is 'Big Bad John' by Jimmy Dean)

Hello everybody! My name is Gabriel and I am your compere for the evening. Thank you all for responding to our advert in the Nazareth Gazette. (I believe the locals call it the Naza Gaza). Now, as you know, we have a vacancy for a fourth gospel writer, and I must say, it's very gratifying to see so many applicants for the job—so many aspiring gospel writers willing to give up their evening to learn the trade.

But before I go any further can I just ask you to raise your hand if your name isn't John? The ad specified that only Johns need apply.

(A hand goes up.)

(Gabriel): So, what's **your** name?

(The hand): Ringo.

(Gabriel): Ringo!? (Addressing the audience in general) … You see, this is precisely why we insisted on a solid, everyday name for our fourth gospel. John is the sort of man you'd let your daughter marry. John is the sort of name you can trust. It oozes reliability. But Ringo!? Who's going to believe the gospel according to Ringo, for Christ's sake!?

(Addressing Ringo): So Ringo, thanks for your interest, but no thanks. We may have something for you in 1,873 years' time.

(Ringo leaves.)

Now, where was I? Ah yes; the purpose of this conference is to give you some introductory training in the dos and don'ts of writing a gospel. For example, later on, Matthew will give a talk on how to script Jesus's conversations so as to make the Pharisees look like a bunch of losers.

But first, we have a very special guest speaker all the way from heaven itself. His bestselling book is of course, The Old Testament, signed copies of which are available in the foyer. And not only that — he's busy writing a blockbusting sequel called, "The Brand-New Testament — this time it's personal". (It's a working title).

He is of course, the third person of the trinity, the ultimate ghost writer himself, please give it up for... **THE HOLY GHOST!**

(Loud applause as the Holy Ghost comes on stage and Gabriel hands over to him).

(Holy Ghost): Thank you, thank you. You're too kind.

Good evening gentlemen and gentlemen. As you may know, being the third person of the trinity, I have a large portfolio which includes not only sleeping with Mary, and killing people who commit the unforgivable sin, but also writing the Bible; and it's in that last capacity that I address you tonight.

My lecture will be on how to write a cracking good miracle story, so if you want to do it right then listen up because I know what I'm talking about. I'll illustrate the kind of thing to avoid by drawing examples from Matthew, Mark, and Luke. They generally toe the line and write decent stuff but, despite my best efforts, even they slip up from time to time.

Now, what's the biggest problem with telling a tall tale?

(Member of the audience): Getting people to believe it.

(HG): Exactly! And miracles are the tallest tales around, so right from the start you've got a credibility problem. How on earth do you get people to believe that the iron laws of the cosmos are casually being shattered on a daily basis by a wandering, unemployed joiner in first century Judaea?

Here's how:

The first thing is to get your miracle stories showcased in the Bible. We're advertising it as the word of God, so they're bound to believe you.

Secondly, you'll have the backing of the church's propaganda machine, brandishing its very own brand of persuasion — know what I mean?

And thirdly, much like advertisers, you'll need to acquire a style of writing that will make people believe anything you tell them, no matter how crazy. The thing is, you've got to tell it in the right way.

Now, the first rule is to make your miracle as routine as possible. Use a deadpan delivery like Jack Dee, or Jack Benny, and tell it in an everyday, matter of fact way.

For example, a blind man comes to Jesus and asks him for healing. Jesus says, "Receive your sight". And the man is healed, end of story. No heavenly trumpets; no flash of light; no special effects. It's as straightforward as making a cup of tea — compare — a man goes into a café and asks for a cup of tea. The waiter says, "Here's your tea". And the man drinks it, end of story. The style makes both stories more believable.

Secondly, make the miracle look easy, as if it was no trouble at all. When Jesus casts out a demon it should read like he's putting the cat out — a bit of futile hissing effortlessly overcome.

Notice also that in the other three gospels Jesus is always portrayed as completely self-confident. He never doubts his ability. His response to disease is always an authoritative command like, "Rise up and walk!" You never hear him say stuff like, "Okay. I'll give it a go. Now let's get you up on your feet and see what happens."

And another thing, you've got to make Jesus look like a natural, so don't include any scenes where he's trying stuff out on the quiet with a couple of paraplegic stooges. Remember, there must be no hint that Jesus needs batting practice.

And don't make the miracle trivial. There are several ways of fouling up here.

For instance, don't surround Jesus with uglies demanding nose jobs, or comb-over baldies wanting the Yul Brynner look. You should also avoid miracles that don't help the victim at all. If you wrote a story where a leper calls out to Jesus, "Lord have mercy!" and Jesus replies, "I will. Here's a bell I've just made from thin air. Ring this.", it just makes him look like an asshole.

And make sure Jesus is never responsible for any half-assed healing. Readers won't be impressed if you have Jesus give a lame man a hip replacement. Of course, and this is aimed at the jokers in the audience, it should go without saying that a miracle should make things better, not worse. If a man with a withered hand begs Jesus to make his hand like the other one, I don't want to read that he ended up with two withered hands.

Avoid using disgusting methods; it doesn't make Jesus look good. Attention gets distracted from Jesus and focuses on the disgusting method. Readers will become suspicious and even start thinking for themselves and we don't want that, do we?

For example, Mark made this mistake when he had Jesus spit in a blind man's face, and follows this up with a half-baked healing, for the man says afterwards that he sees men walking around as trees. It's only after Jesus tries again that the man can see properly. Now, what went wrong here is that readers start to wonder whether there was some chemical in Jesus's saliva that was actually responsible for the cure. And why did it take two instalments? They'll start to wonder why Jesus didn't simply avoid all the mumbo jumbo, and just tell the man to see.

But be careful you don't go over the top in the other direction and hype it up too much. I'm sure Matthew won't mind me telling you how he fouled up. You see, instead of leaving well enough alone by having just Jesus raised from the dead, he couldn't resist the thought of having a few hundred of his dead followers rise up along with him. That was bad enough, but he went even further and had them strolling around Jerusalem in broad daylight. He should have quit while he was ahead, but oh no, he had to go for a spectacular finale. And what was the result? Instead of the focus remaining on the glorious resurrection of the Son of God, the reader is left stunned by a scene straight out of a zombie movie. We've had Matthew on the carpet for that little stunt, and we're determined not to let another story like that slip through.

Don't get me wrong, we in the trinity are all for resurrection stories, but you need to box clever. No one wants to be bumping into dead relatives when they're doing their shopping.

My next piece of advice is for those of you who have a strong sense of humour. Don't have Jesus performing miracles just for a laugh. **You** might find it funny to have him turn water into diesel instead of wine, or to give the Pharisees piles, but resist the temptation. Have you noticed, there's not a single gag in any of the other three gospels? We want to keep it that way. You can say that Jesus wept, was tired, or even that he was angry, but never say things like, "Jesus smirked, giggled, or guffawed." It undercuts the solemnity needed for people to believe. Faith is a **mood.**

And this is why you shouldn't have him doing miracles in an undignified manner. Look at the story of Jesus walking on the water. This is how it should be written because readers expect God to walk at a dignified pace. But if you have him doing handstands, and backflips in the middle of the Sea of Galilee you turn him into a circus performer: Jesus the holy acrobat. This saps credulity, and we must keep our readers credulous at all costs.

The lecture is drawing to a close, but before I finish, I'd like to point out one last thing to avoid. Whatever you do, don't have Jesus doing miracles that are purely self-serving. It makes him look bad. There's a good example of this mistake in Matthew's gospel where Jesus is accused of not paying his taxes. So to pay his tax bill, and satisfy the Temple revenue boys, he miraculously produces the money from a fish's mouth. It's actually a bit weirder than this, because he tells

Peter to go and catch a fish and predicts that the fish will have the money.

The problem here is that people tend to take a rather jaundiced view of this kind of tax dodge. They'll think it very handy to have a miracle up your sleeve when the boys from the Inland Revenue come calling, instead of having to work for a living like everybody else. And why not make it even handier by producing the coins from behind Peter's ear like a proper magician instead of sending him on a fishing trip? This miracle benefitted no one but Jesus… oh, and the tax man.

Let me leave you with one final thought. Avoid humour at all costs. It's the deadliest enemy of faith. These mistakes I've talked about—do you know what makes them mistakes? What it is they all have in common? They open the door to laughter. Satire, slapstick, wit, farce; these undermine our attempts to get people to obey and believe without question.

So if you want to be a successful gospel writer, whatever you do, kill the joy of humour within you. Let your motto be: **FUNNY FUCKS FAITH!**

Thank you all very much.

(Standing ovation begins as Gabriel comes back on and shouts to the audience:

Let's hear it for the Ghostess with the mostess!)

(Applause continues as the Holy Ghost walks off to the strains of 'You Sexy Thing' 'by Hot Chocolate.)

APPENDIX

All of the biblical texts copied here are taken from the New Revised Standard Version of the Bible, but feel free to use whatever translation suits you.

I was born under a wandering star.

The Relevant biblical texts:

Matthew 1:18 – 2:23 and Luke 2:1–20

Matt.1:18 Now the birth of Jesus the Messiah took place in this way. When his mother Mary had been engaged to Joseph, but before they lived together, she was found to be with child from the Holy Spirit.

19 Her husband Joseph, being a righteous man and unwilling to expose her to public disgrace, planned to dismiss her quietly.

20 But just when he had resolved to do this, an angel of the Lord appeared to him in a dream and said, 'Joseph, son of David, do not be afraid to take Mary as your wife, for the child conceived in her is from the Holy Spirit.

21 She will bear a son, and you are to name him Jesus, for he will save his people from their sins.'

22 All this took place to fulfil what had been spoken by the Lord through the prophet:

23 'Look, the virgin shall conceive and bear a son, and they shall name him Emmanuel', which means, 'God is with us.'

24 When Joseph awoke from sleep, he did as the angel of the Lord commanded him: he took her as his wife,

25 but had no marital relations with her until she had borne a son, and he named him Jesus.

2:1 In the time of King Herod, after Jesus was born in Bethlehem of Judea, wise men from the East came to Jerusalem,

2 asking, 'Where is the child who has been born king of the Jews? For we observed his star at its rising, and have come to pay him homage.'

3 When King Herod heard this, he was frightened, and all Jerusalem with him;

4 and calling together all the chief priests and scribes of the people, he inquired of them where the Messiah was to be born.

5 They told him, 'In Bethlehem of Judea; for so it has been written by the prophet:

6 'And you, Bethlehem, in the land of Judah, are by no means least among the rulers of Judah; for from you shall come a ruler who is to shepherd my people Israel.'

7 Then Herod secretly called for the wise men and learned from them the exact time when the star had appeared.

8 Then he sent them to Bethlehem, saying, 'Go and search diligently for the child; and when you have found him, bring me word so that I may also go and pay him homage.'

9 When they had heard the king, they set out; and there, ahead of them, went the star that they had seen at its rising, until it stopped over the place where the child was.

10 When they saw that the star had stopped, they were overwhelmed with joy.

11 On entering the house, they saw the child with Mary his mother; and they knelt down and paid him homage. Then, opening their treasure-chests, they offered him gifts of gold, frankincense, and myrrh.

12 And having been warned in a dream not to return to Herod, they left for their own country by another road.

13 Now after they had left, an angel of the Lord appeared to Joseph in a dream and said, 'Get up, take the child and his mother, and flee to Egypt, and remain there until I tell you; for Herod is about to search for the child, to destroy him.'

14 Then Joseph got up, took the child and his mother by night, and went to Egypt,

15 and remained there until the death of Herod. This was to fulfil what had been spoken by the Lord through the prophet, 'Out of Egypt I have called my son.'

16 When Herod saw that he had been tricked by the wise men, he was infuriated, and he sent and killed all the children in and around Bethlehem who were two years old or under, according to the time that he had learned from the wise men.

17 Then was fulfilled what had been spoken through the prophet Jeremiah:

18 'A voice was heard in Ramah, wailing and loud lamentation, Rachel weeping for her children; she refused to be consoled, because they are no more.'

19 When Herod died, an angel of the Lord suddenly appeared in a dream to Joseph in Egypt and said,

20 'Get up, take the child and his mother, and go to the land of Israel, for those who were seeking the child's life are dead.'

21 Then Joseph got up, took the child and his mother, and went to the land of Israel.

22 But when he heard that Archelaus was ruling over Judea in place of his father Herod, he was afraid to go there. And after being warned in a dream, he went away to the district of Galilee.

23 There he made his home in a town called Nazareth, so that what had been spoken through the prophets might be fulfilled, 'He will be called a Nazarean.'

Luke. 2: 1–20

Luke. 2:1 In those days a decree went out from Emperor Augustus that all the world should be registered.

2 This was the first registration and was taken while Quirinius was governor of Syria.

3 All went to their own towns to be registered.

4 Joseph also went from the town of Nazareth in Galilee to Judea, to the city of David called Bethlehem, because he was descended from the house and family of David.

5 He went to be registered with Mary, to whom he was engaged and who was expecting a child.

6 While they were there, the time came for her to deliver her child.

7 And she gave birth to her firstborn son and wrapped him in bands of cloth, and laid him in a manger, because there was no place for them in the inn.

8 In that region there were shepherds living in the fields, keeping watch over their flock by night.

9 Then an angel of the Lord stood before them, and the glory of the Lord shone around them, and they were terrified.

10 But the angel said to them, 'Do not be afraid; for see — I am bringing you good news of great joy for all the people:

11 To you is born this day in the city of David a Saviour, who is the Messiah, the Lord.

12 This will be a sign for you: you will find a child wrapped in bands of cloth and lying in a manger.'

13 And suddenly there was with the angel a multitude of the heavenly host, praising God and saying,

14 Glory to God in the highest heaven, and on earth peace among those whom he favours!'

15 When the angels had left them and gone into heaven, the shepherds said to one another, 'Let us go now to Bethlehem and see this thing that has taken place, which the Lord had made known to us.'

16 So they went with haste and found Mary and Joseph, and the child lying in the manger.

17 When they saw this, they made known what had been told them about this child;

18 and all who heard it were amazed at what the shepherds told them.

19 But Mary treasured all these words and pondered them in her heart.

20 The shepherds returned, glorifying and praising God for all they had heard and seen, as it had been told them.

The Chianti-Christ

Relevant biblical text:

John. 2: 1 – 11

2:1 On the third day there was a wedding in Cana of Galilee, and the mother of Jesus was there.

2 Jesus and his disciples had also been invited to the wedding.

3 When the wine gave out, the mother of Jesus said to him, 'They have no wine.'

4 And Jesus said to her, 'Woman, what concern is that to you and to me? My hour has not yet come.'

5 His mother said to the servants, 'Do whatever he tells you.'

6 Now standing there were six stone water-jars for the Jewish rites of purification, each holding twenty or thirty gallons.

7 Jesus said to them, 'Fill the jars with water.' And they filled them up to the brim.

8 He said to them, 'Now draw some out, and take it to the chief steward.' So they took it.

9 When the steward tasted the water that had become wine, and did not know where it came from (though the servants who had drawn the water knew), the steward called the bridegroom

    10 and said to him, 'Everyone serves the good wine first, and then the inferior wine after the guests have become drunk. But you have kept the good wine until now.'

    11 Jesus did this, the first of his signs, in Cana of Galilee, and revealed his glory; and his disciples believed in him.

Anti-Gentile Jesus Meek and Mild.

Relevant biblical texts:

Matthew. 15: 21 – 28 and Mark. 7: 24 – 30

Matt. 15:21 Jesus left that place and went away to the district of Tyre and Sidon.

22 Just then a Canaanite woman from that region came out and started shouting, 'Have mercy on me, Lord, Son of David; my daughter is tormented by a demon.'

23 But he did not answer her at all. And his disciples came and urged him, saying, 'Send her away, for she keeps shouting after us.'

24 He answered, 'I was sent only to the lost sheep of the house of Israel.'

25 But she came and knelt before him, saying, 'Lord, help me.'

26 He answered, 'It is not fair to take the children's food and throw it to the dogs.'

27 She said, 'Yes, Lord, yet even the dogs eat the crumbs that fall from their masters' table.'

28 Then Jesus answered her, 'Woman, great is your faith! Let it be done for you as you wish.' And her daughter was healed instantly.

Mark. 7: 24 – 30

Mark. 7:24 From there he set out and went away to the region of Tyre. He entered a house and did not want anyone to know he was there. Yet he could not escape notice,

25 but a woman whose little daughter had an unclean spirit immediately heard about him, and she came and bowed down at his feet.

26 Now the woman was a Gentile, of Syrophoenician origin. She begged him to cast the demon out of her daughter.

27 He said to her, 'Let the children be fed first, for it is not fair to take the children's food and throw it to the dogs.'

28 But she answered him, 'Sir, even the dogs under the table eat the children's crumbs.'

29 Then he said to her, 'For saying that, you may go — the demon has left your daughter.'

30 So she went home, found the child lying on the bed, and the demon gone.

The Deadwood Sage.

Relevant biblical texts:

Matthew. 21: 18 – 22 and Mark. 11: 12 – 24.

Matt.21: 18 In the morning, when he returned to the city, he was hungry.

19 And seeing a fig tree by the side of the road, he went to it and found nothing at all on it but leaves. Then he said to it, 'May no fruit ever come from you again!' And the fig tree withered at once.

20 When the disciples saw it, they were amazed, saying, 'How did the fig tree wither at once?'

21 Jesus answered them, 'Truly I tell you, if you have faith and do not doubt, not only will you do what has been done to the fig tree, but even if you say to this mountain, "Be lifted up and thrown into the sea", it will be done.

22 Whatever you ask for in prayer with faith, you will receive.'

Mark. 11: 12 – 24

Mark.11: 12 On the following day, when they came from Bethany, he was hungry.

13 Seeing in the distance a fig tree in leaf, he went to see whether perhaps he would find anything on it. When he came

140

to it, he found nothing but leaves, for it was not the season for figs.

14 He said to it, 'May no one ever eat fruit from you again.' and his disciples heard it.

15 Then they came to Jerusalem. And he entered the temple and began to drive out those who were selling and those who were buying in the temple, and he overturned the tables of the money-changers and the seats of those who sold doves;

16 and he would not allow anyone to carry anything through the temple.

17 He was teaching and saying, 'Is it not written, "My house shall be called a house of prayer for all the nations"? But you have made it a den of robbers.'

18 And when the chief priests and the scribes heard it, they kept looking for a way to kill him; for they were afraid of him, because the whole crowd was spellbound by his teaching.

19 And when evening came, Jesus and his disciples went out of the city.

20 In the morning as they passed by, they saw the fig tree withered away to its roots.

21 Then Peter remembered and said to him, 'Rabbi, look! The fig tree that you cursed has withered.'

22 Jesus answered them, 'Have faith in God.

23 Truly I tell you, if you say to this mountain, "Be taken up and thrown into the sea", and if you do not doubt in your heart, but believe that what you say will come to pass, it will be done for you.

24 So I tell you, whatever you ask for in prayer, believe that you have received it, and it will be yours.'

God's Boy Ahoy!

Relevant biblical texts:

Matthew. 14: 21 – 34 (verses 13 – 21 cover the feeding of the 5000)

Mark. 6: 44 – 53 (verses 33 – 43 cover the feeding of the 5000)

John. 6: 16 – 21 (verses 1 – 15 cover the feeding of the 5000)

Luke. 9: 10 – 17 covers the feeding of the 5000, but verse 10 locates this miracle at the town of **Bethsaida**. NB. Luke does not mention Jesus walking on water.

Luke. 9: 10 – 11, and 14 – 17

10 – 11 *On their return the apostles told Jesus all they had done. He took them with him and withdrew privately to a city called Bethsaida. When the crowds found out about it, they followed him…*

14 – 17 *… there were about five thousand men. And he said to his disciples, 'Make them sit down in groups of about fifty each.' They did so and made them all sit down. And taking the five loaves and the two fish, he looked up to heaven, and blessed and broke them, and gave them to the disciples to set*

before the crowd, and all ate and were filled. What was left over was gathered up, twelve baskets of broken pieces.

Matthew. 14: 21 – 34

Matthew. 14: 21 *And those who ate were about five thousand men, besides women and children.*

22 Immediately he made the disciples get into the boat and go on ahead to the other side, while he dismissed the crowds.

23 And after he had dismissed the crowds, he went up the mountain by himself to pray. When evening came, he was there alone,

24 but by this time the boat, battered by the waves, was far from the land, for the wind was against them.

25 And early in the morning he came walking towards them on the lake.

26 But when the disciples saw him walking on the lake, they were terrified, saying, 'It is a ghost!' And they cried out in fear.

27 But immediately Jesus spoke to them and said, 'Take heart, it is I; do not be afraid.'

28 Peter answered him, 'Lord, if it is you, command me to come to you on the water.'

29 He said, 'Come.' So Peter got out of the boat, started walking on the water, and came towards Jesus.

30 But when he noticed the strong wind, he became frightened, and beginning to sink, he cried out, 'Lord, save me!'

31 Jesus immediately reached out his hand and caught him, saying to him, 'You of little faith, why did you doubt?'

32 When they got into the boat, the wind ceased.

33 And those in the boat worshipped him, saying, 'Truly you are the Son of God.'

34 When they crossed over, they came to land at Gennesaret.

Mark. 6: 44 – 53

Mark. 6: 44 Those who had eaten the loaves numbered five thousand men.

45 Immediately he made his disciples get into the boat and go on ahead to the other side, to Bethsaida, while he dismissed the crowd.

46 After saying farewell to them, he went up on the mountain to pray.

47 When evening came, the boat was out on the lake, and he was alone on the land.

48 When he saw that they were straining at the oars against an adverse wind, he came towards them early in the morning, walking on the lake. He intended to pass them by.

49 But when they saw him walking on the lake, they thought it was a ghost and cried out;

50 for they all saw him and were terrified. But immediately he spoke to them and said, 'Take heart, it is I; do not be afraid.'

51 Then he got into the boat with them and the wind ceased. And they were utterly astounded,

52 for they did not understand about the loaves, but their hearts were hardened.

53 When they had crossed over, they came to land at Gennesaret and moored the boat.

John. 6: 16 – 21

John. 6:16 When evening came, his disciples went down to the lake,

17 got into a boat, and started across the lake to Capernaum. It was now dark, and Jesus had not yet come to them.

18 The lake became rough because a strong wind was blowing.

19 When they had rowed about three or four miles, they saw Jesus walking on the lake and coming near the boat, and they were terrified.

20 But he said to them, 'It is I; do not be afraid.'

21 Then they wanted to take him into the boat, and immediately the boat reached the land towards which they were going.

The Animal Rights Inactivist.

Relevant biblical texts: Mark. 5: 1 – 20, Luke. 8: 26 – 39,
Matthew. 8: 28 – 34

Mark. 5: 1 – 20

*Mark. 5: 1 They came to the other side of the lake, to the
country of the Gerasenes.*

*2 And when he had stepped out of the boat, immediately a
man out of the tombs with an unclean spirit met him.*

*3 He lived among the tombs; and no one could restrain
him any more, even with a chain;*

*4 for he had often been restrained with shackles and
chains, but the chains he wrenched apart, and the shackles he
broke in pieces; and no one had the strength to subdue him.*

*5 Night and day among the tombs and on the mountains,
he was always howling and bruising himself with stones.*

*6 When he saw Jesus from a distance, he ran and bowed
down before him;*

*7 and he shouted at the top of his voice, 'What have you
to do with me, Jesus, Son of the Most High God? I adjure you
by God, do not torment me.'*

*8 For he had said to him, 'Come out of the man, you
unclean spirit!'*

9 Then Jesus asked him, 'What is your name?' He replied, 'My name is Legion; for we are many.'

10 He begged him earnestly not to send them out of the country.

11 Now there on the hillside a great herd of swine was feeding;

12 and the unclean spirits begged him, 'Send us into the swine; let us enter them.'

13 So he gave them permission. And the unclean spirits came out and entered the swine; and the herd, numbering about 2000, rushed down the steep bank into the lake, and were drowned in the lake.

14 The swineherds ran off and told it in the city and in the country. Then people came to see what it was that had happened.

15 They came to Jesus and saw the demoniac sitting there, clothed and in his right mind, the very man who had had the legion; and they were afraid.

16 Those who had seen what had happened to the demoniac and to the swine reported it.

17 Then they began to beg Jesus to leave their neighbourhood.

18 And as he was getting into the boat, the man who had been possessed by the demons begged him that he might be with him.

19 But Jesus refused, and said to him, 'Go home to your friends, and tell them how much the Lord has done for you, and what mercy he has shown you.

20 And he went away and began to proclaim in the Decapolis how much Jesus had done for him; and everyone was amazed.

Luke. 8: 26 – 39

Luke. 8: 26 Then they arrived at the country of the Gerasenes, which is opposite Galilee.

27 As he stepped out on land, a man of the city who had demons met him. For a long time, he had worn no clothes, and he did not live in a house but in the tombs.

28 When he saw Jesus, he fell down before him and shouted at the top of his voice, 'What have you to do with me, Jesus, Son of the Most High God? I beg you, do not torment me' —

29 for Jesus had commanded the unclean spirit to come out of the man. (For many times it had seized him; he was kept under guard and bound with chains and shackles, but he would break the bonds and be driven by the demon into the wilds.)

30 Jesus then asked him, 'What is your name?' He said, 'Legion'; for many demons had entered into him.

31 They begged him not to order them to go back into the abyss.

32 Now there on the hillside a large herd of swine was feeding; and the demons begged Jesus to let them enter these. So he gave them permission.

33 Then the demons came out of the man and entered the swine, and the herd rushed down the steep bank into the lake and was drowned.

34 When the swineherds saw what had happened, they ran off and told it in the city and in the country.

35 Then people came out to see what had happened, and when they came to Jesus, they found the man from whom the demons had gone sitting at the feet of Jesus, clothed and in his right mind. And they were afraid.

36 Those who had seen it told them how the one who had been possessed by demons had been healed.

37 Then all the people of the surrounding country of the Gerasenes asked Jesus to leave them; for they were seized with great fear. So he got into the boat and returned.

38 The man from whom the demons had gone begged that he might be with him; but Jesus sent him away, saying,

39 'Return to your home, and declare how much God has done for you.' So he went away, proclaiming throughout the city how much Jesus had done for him.

Matthew. 8: 28 – 34

Matthew. 8: 28 When he came to the other side, to the country of the Gadarenes, two demoniacs coming out of the tombs met him. They were so fierce that no one could pass that way.

29 Suddenly they shouted, 'What have you to do with us, Son of God? Have you come here to torment us before the time?'

30 Now a large herd of swine was feeding at some distance from them.

31 The demons begged him, 'If you cast us out, send us into the herd of swine.'

32 And he said to them, 'Go!' So they came out and entered the swine; and suddenly, the whole herd rushed down the steep bank into the lake and perished in the water.

33 The swineherds ran off, and, on going into the town, they told the whole story about what had happened to the demoniacs.

34 Then the whole town came out to meet Jesus; and when they saw him, they begged him to leave their neighbourhood. And after getting into a boat he crossed the water and came to his own town.

Rocketman

Relevant biblical texts:
    Luke. 24: 1 – 53
    Acts. 1: 1 – 11

Luke. 24: 1 – 53

Luke. 24: 1 But on the first day of the week, at early dawn, they came to the tomb, taking the spices that they had prepared.

2 They found the stone rolled away from the tomb,

3 but when they went in, they did not find the body.

4 While they were perplexed about this, suddenly two men in dazzling clothes stood beside them.

5 The women were terrified and bowed their faces to the ground, but the men said to them, 'Why do you look for the living among the dead? He is not here, but has risen.

6 Remember how he told you, while he was still in Galilee,

7 that the Son of Man must be handed over to sinners, and be crucified, and on the third day rise again.'

8 Then they remembered his words,

9 and returning from the tomb, they told all this to the eleven and to all the rest.

10 Now it was Mary Magdalene, Joanna, Mary the mother of James, and the other women with them who told this to the apostles.

11 But these words seemed to them an idle tale, and they did not believe them.

12 But Peter got up and ran to the tomb; stooping and looking in, he saw the linen cloths by themselves; then he went home, amazed at what had happened.

13 Now on that same day two of them were going to a village called Emmaus, about seven miles from Jerusalem,

14 and talking with each other about all these things that had happened.

15 While they were talking and discussing, Jesus himself came near and went with them,

16 but their eyes were kept from recognizing him.

17 And he said to them, 'What are you discussing with each other while you walk along?' They stood still, looking sad.

18 Then one of them, whose name was Cleopas, answered him, 'Are you the only stranger in Jerusalem who does not know the things that have taken place there in these days?'

19 He asked them, 'What things?' They replied, 'The things about Jesus of Nazareth, who was a prophet mighty in deed and word before God and all the people,

20 and how our chief priests and leaders handed him over to be condemned to death and crucified him.

21 But we had hoped that he was the one to redeem Israel. Yes, and besides all this, it is now the third day since these things took place.

22 Moreover, some women of our group astounded us. They were at the tomb early this morning,

23 and when they did not find his body there, they came back and told us that they had indeed seen a vision of angels who said that he was alive.

24 Some of those who were with us went to the tomb and found it just as the women had said; but they did not see him.'

25 Then he said to them, 'Oh how foolish you are, and how slow of heart to believe all that the prophets have declared!

26 Was it not necessary that the Messiah should suffer these things and then enter into his glory?'

27 Then beginning with Moses and all the prophets, he interpreted to them the things about himself in all the scriptures.

28 As they came near the village to which they were going, he walked ahead as if he were going on.

29 But they urged him strongly, saying, 'Stay with us, because it is almost evening and the day is now nearly over.' So he went in to stay with them.

30 When he was at the table with them, he took bread, blessed and broke it, and gave it to them.

31 Then their eyes were opened, and they recognized him; and he vanished from their sight.

32 They said to each other, 'Were not our hearts burning within us while he was talking to us on the road, while he was opening the Scriptures to us?'

33 That same hour they got up and returned to Jerusalem; and they found the eleven and their companions gathered together.

34 They were saying, 'The Lord has risen indeed, and he has appeared to Simon!'

35 Then they told what had happened on the road, and how he had been made known to them in the breaking of bread.

36 While they were talking about this, Jesus himself stood among them and said to them, 'Peace be with you.'

37 They were startled and terrified, and thought that they were seeing a ghost.

38 He said to them, 'Why are you frightened, and why do doubts arise in your hearts?

39 Look at my hands and my feet; see that it is I myself. Touch me and see; for a ghost does not have flesh and bones as you see that I have.'

40 And when he had said this, he showed them his hands and his feet.

41 While in their joy they were disbelieving and still wondering, he said to them, 'Have you anything here to eat?'

42 They gave him a piece of broiled fish,

43 and he took it and ate in their presence.

44 Then he said to them, 'These are my words that I spoke to you while I was still with you — that everything written about me in the law of Moses, the prophets, and the psalms must be fulfilled.'

45 Then he opened their minds to understand the scriptures,

46 and he said to them, 'Thus it is written, that the Messiah is to suffer and to rise from the dead on the third day,

47 and that repentance and forgiveness of sins is to be proclaimed in his name to all nations, beginning from Jerusalem.

48 You are witnesses of these things.

49 And see, I am sending upon you what my Father promised; so stay here in the city until you have been clothed with power from on high.'

50 Then he led them out as far as Bethany, and, lifting up his hands, he blessed them.

51 While he was blessing them, he withdrew from them and was carried up into heaven.

52 And they worshipped him, and returned to Jerusalem with great joy;

53 and they were continually in the temple blessing God.

Acts. 1: 1 – 11

Acts. 1:1 In the first book, Theophilus, I wrote about all that Jesus did and taught from the beginning

2 until the day when he was taken up to heaven, after giving instructions through the Holy Spirit to the apostles whom he had chosen.

3 After his suffering he presented himself alive to them by many convincing proofs, appearing to them over the course of forty days and speaking about the kingdom of God.

4 While staying with them, he ordered them not to leave Jerusalem, but to wait there for the promise of the Father. 'This', he said, 'is what you have heard from me;

5 for John baptized with water, but you will be baptized with the Holy Spirit not many days from now.

6 So when they had come together, they asked him, 'Lord, is this the time when you will restore the kingdom to Israel?'

7 He replied, 'It is not for you to know the times or periods that the Father has set by his own authority.

8 But you will receive power when the Holy Spirit has come upon you; and you will be my witnesses in Jerusalem, in all Judea and Samaria, and to the ends of the earth.'

9 When he had said this, as they were watching, he was lifted up, and a cloud took him out of their sight.

10 While he was going and they were gazing up towards heaven, suddenly two men in white robes stood by them.

11 They said, 'Men of Galilee, why do you stand looking up towards heaven? This Jesus, who has been taken up from you into heaven, will come in the same way as you saw him go into heaven.'

Moneytheism

Relevant biblical text:

Acts. 4: 32 – 5: 11

Acts. 4:32 Now the whole group of those who believed were of one heart and soul, and no one claimed private ownership of any possessions, but everything they owned was held in common.

33 With great power the apostles gave their testimony to the resurrection of the Lord Jesus, and great grace was upon them all.

34 There was not a needy person among them, for as many as owned lands or houses sold them and brought the proceeds of what was sold.

35 They laid it at the apostles' feet, and it was distributed to each as any had need.

36 There was a Levite, a native of Cyprus, Joseph, to whom the apostles gave the name Barnabas (which means 'son of encouragement').

37 He sold a field that belonged to him, then brought the money and laid it at the apostles' feet.

Acts. 5:1 But a man named Ananias, with the consent of his wife Sapphira, sold a piece of property;

2 with his wife's knowledge, he kept back some of the proceeds, and brought only a part and laid it at the apostles' feet.

3 'Ananias,' Peter asked, 'why has Satan filled your heart to lie to the Holy Spirit and to keep back part of the proceeds of the land?

4 While it remained unsold, did it not remain your own? And after it was sold, were not the proceeds at your disposal? How is it that you have contrived this deed in your heart? You did not lie to us but to God!'

5 Now when Ananias heard these words, he fell down and died. And great fear seized all who heard of it.

6 The young men came and wrapped up his body, then carried him out and buried him.

7 After an interval of about three hours his wife came in, not knowing what had happened.

8 Peter said to her, 'Tell me whether you and your husband sold the land for such and such a price.' And she said, 'Yes, that was the price.'

9 Then Peter said to her, 'How is it that you have agreed together to put the Spirit of the Lord to the test? Look, the feet of those who have buried your husband are at the door, and they will carry you out.'

10 Immediately she fell down at his feet and died. When the young men came in, they found her dead, so they carried her out and buried her beside her husband.

11 And great fear seized the whole church and all who heard of these things.

How To Write A Cracking Good Miracle Story

Relevant biblical texts:

Matthew. 17: 24 – 27

24 When they reached Capernaum, the collectors of the temple tax came to Peter and said, 'Does your teacher not pay the temple tax?'

25 He said, 'Yes, he does.' And when he came home, Jesus spoke of it first, asking, 'What do you think, Simon? From whom do kings of the earth take toll or tribute? From their children or from others?'

26 When Peter said, 'From others', Jesus said to him, 'Then the children are free.

27 However, so that we do not give offence to them, go to the lake and cast a hook; take the first fish that comes up; and when you open its mouth you will find a coin; take that and give it to them for you and me.'

Matthew. 28: 50 – 53

50 Then Jesus cried again with a loud voice and breathed his last.

51 At that moment the curtain of the temple was torn in two, from top to bottom. The earth shook, and the rocks were split.

52 The tombs also were opened, and many bodies of the saints who had fallen asleep were raised.

53 After his resurrection they came out of the tombs and entered the holy city and appeared to many.

Mark. 8: 22 – 25

22 They came to Bethsaida. Some people brought a blind man to him and begged him to touch him.

23 He took the blind man by the hand and led him out of the village; and when he had put saliva on his eyes and laid his hands on him, he asked him, 'Can you see anything?'

24 And the man looked up and said, 'I can see people, but they look like trees, walking.'

25 Then Jesus laid his hands on his eyes again; and he looked intently and his sight was restored, and he saw everything clearly.